How-To Books: Writing to Teach Others

Lucy Calkins, Laurie Pessah, and Elizabeth Moore

Photography by Peter Cunningham

HEINEMANN ◆ PORTSMOUTH, NH

This book is dedicated to Hannah and Lily, who remind us every day how to marvel at capped acorns, at swirls of frost in the snow.

Heinemann
361 Hanover Street
Portsmouth, NH 03801–3912
www.heinemann.com

Offices and agents throughout the world

© 2013 by Lucy Calkins, Laurie Pessah, and Elizabeth Moore

The authors and publisher wish to thank those who have generously given permission to reprint borrowed material:

Reprinted with the permission of Little Simon, an imprint of Simon & Schuster Children's Publishing Division from *My First Soccer Game* by Alyssa Satin Capucilli. Copyright © 2011 Alyssa Satin Capucilli.

Cataloging-in-Publication data is on file with the Library of Congress.

ISBN-13: 978-0-325-04722-5

Production: Elizabeth Valway, David Stirling, and Abigail M. Heim
Cover and interior designs: Jenny Jensen Greenleaf
Series includes photographs by Peter Cunningham, Nadine Baldasare, and Elizabeth Dunford
Composition: Publishers' Design and Production Services, Inc.
Manufacturing: Steve Bernier

Printed in the United States of America on acid-free paper
20 19 18 17 16 VP 10 9 8 7 6

Acknowledgments

THE THREE OF US are indebted first and most to the community of educators who comprise the Teachers College Reading and Writing Project. All the people who teach and think and write and invent together at the Project—and who have done so over the years—have lent their wisdom to this effort. Each little bit of this book deserves a footnote. The architecture of the minilesson: that's a gift from a think tank that worked together more than a decade ago. The fresh ideas about working with partners: those ideas have a little bit of Kathy Collins sewn into them. The various scaffolds that we provide and remove: thanks to Shanna Schwartz for the conversations out of which these emerge. The cyclical nature of the unit, with its bends in the road: thanks to the upper-grade coauthors for that structure to units. Everything in this book benefits from these people and countless others who comprise the Teachers College Reading and Writing Project community.

There are two people in that community who have been helpful for this book in very specific ways. We are especially grateful to Amanda Hartman, our associate director, and to Julia Mooney, our writer in residence.

The Project staff meet together every Thursday, and many of our insights have grown out of those Thursday study groups. But much of the most intense, most poignant, most surprising insights are developed not around the table at the Project but instead, in schools and classrooms. We're especially grateful to the schools that helped us pilot the latest iteration of this unit. Thanks to Gina Faust, principal extraordinaire of Roosevelt School in Oyster Bay, Long Island, and to Chris Bartell, Carrie Ryles, and Marisa Carnesi, who opened their doors and joined us in the thinking. Many thanks to Molly Wang, principal at PS 173 in Queens, and Ilene Savoy, whose classroom is always a pleasure to learn from.

This book would not be what it is without the incredible staff at Heinemann who put heart and soul into making it the best book it could possibly be. Zoë White Ryder served as editor, and in that capacity she did far more than edit. She rewrote, coached, guided, and celebrated. We're especially grateful that she brought her deep love of kindergartners to this book and kept the children foremost in her mind as she worked with us. Teva Blair organized the entire effort, keeping all the writers and all the books on track. Elizabeth Valway, Jean Lawler, Abby Heim, and the rest of the production editors and *first*hand team members, worked their magic in so many ways and kept us all in good cheer. And, of course, we are grateful to Kate Montgomery, who has been the leading light at Heinemann for us for many years and who kept the three of us company as we worked on this endeavor together.

The class described in this unit is a composite class, with children and partnerships of children gleaned from classrooms in very different contexts, then put together here. We wrote the units this way both to bring you a wide array of wonderful, quirky, various children and also to illustrate for you the predictable (and unpredictable) situations and responses this unit has created in classrooms across the nation and world.

—Lucy, Laurie, and Beth

Contents

Welcome to the Unit

IN MANY CASES, it will be you who will introduce your kids to the world of creating written language. This is an enormously important responsibility. You will convey to children that little marks on the page tell stories, carry jokes, give orders, and change the world. And you will guide each child in your care to believe that those little marks on the page will be a source of joy and laughter, friendship, and power.

Kindergarten teachers and caregivers have long known that young children are capable of amazing work when given time, supplies, and opportunity. For decades, kindergartners in writing workshops across the country have been producing information texts that meet the expectations that are now officially coded in the Common Core State Standards. By the end of kindergarten, children are supposed to be able to "use a combination of drawing, dictating, and writing to compose informative/explanatory texts in which they name what they are writing about and supply some information about the topic" (W.K.2). Under the umbrella of information writing, there are many types of writing: from expository (all-about) books, to lists, to field guides, feature articles, and more. How-to, or procedural writing, is one type of information writing. We think it is especially appropriate for early kindergartners.

The work at the heart of this unit is right up kindergartners' alley. The genre of how-to writing weaves together drawing (with labels, of course) and writing, and it has a hands-on, action-oriented feel. To do this work, kindergartners alternate between doing (often dramatizing), drawing, and writing. Because children at this age are movers and shakers, dancers and climbers, dirt-diggers and puddle-jumpers, the active try-it-out nature of the unit spurs them to write more. Look around the classroom as children write how-to books, and you'll see one child shifting between folding paper to make a flower and recording her steps and another rereading a friend's "How to Do a Headstand," mentally (and sometimes physically) reenacting the stunt as a way to comprehend the draft and as a way to find missing information for the writer to add.

The actual writing that children do when writing procedural texts is heavily scaffolded. They break each procedure into steps and then act out or envision the first step, record it, then proceed to act out or envision the next step. Some children will have begun to approximate Common Core expectations for first or second grade, which include providing some sense of closure (W.1.2) or writing to introduce the topic (W.2.2).

Once writers have reached the end of the procedure they are detailing, they reread to see if it clearly explains the actual process. They will return to the text to clarify and enrich, again and again. While doing this, it is likely that they'll work on introductions and conclusions.

Although this unit clearly meets the writing standards for information writing, it also supports other standards. When five- and six-year-olds write anything, a good deal of their focus is on the act of writing itself: on sounding out words, segmenting them, distinguishing sounds, matching sound to letter. The unit, then, supports children's abilities to use a repertoire of strategies to spell words using, at the very least, the basic CCSS requirement of "a letter or letters for most consonant and short-vowel sounds" (CCSS L K.2.c). Children will also receive lots of coaching in learning to "capitalize the first word in a sentence and the pronoun *I*" (CCSS L.K.2.a) and in understanding "that words are separated by spaces in print" (CCSS RF K.1.c). As children practice saying words slowly to hear all of the sounds so that they can write them, they are simultaneously "learning basic knowledge of letter-sound correspondences by producing the primary sounds for each consonant, and to associate the long and short sounds with common spellings for the five major vowels" (CCSS

RF K.3.a-b). As children learn to use the word wall as a resource for spelling high-frequency words, they are also learning to "read common high frequency words by sight" (CCSS K.3.c). Reading and writing will be inextricably linked in this unit; every move that a beginning writer makes has payoff for that child's work as a reader.

The Common Core suggestion that students' total writing time for narrative, opinion, and information writing be equal and the suggestion that information writing needs to occur *across the entire day* means that it is especially important that the information writing children do during the writing workshop transfer to other content areas. This unit provides opportunities for children to write how-to texts relating to the science and social studies units they are studying. Science texts are filled with instructions for experiments and with procedural writing about investigations. To read these texts or to write lab reports, children rely on knowledge of procedural writing. Then, too, because the unit supports students transferring their skills to new disciplines, the unit supports the type of strategic work that Webb's Depth of Knowledge (DOK) refers to as "extended thinking." That is, this is both child-centered and challenging work!

OVERVIEW OF THE UNIT

There are four bends in the road of this unit. Although the instructional focus changes a bit as your children progress through the unit, you will always want to expect that they are continuing to write lots and lots of how-to texts. To give you a picture of the unit, imagine for starters that each of your children is writing about three how-to books during each of the bends in the road of this unit, save for the last bend. The books will become longer and more developed as children become more proficient, but from the start, each book will probably contain at least five pages. Those pages, of course, can contain more or less writing—and for some, it may feel like a stretch to describe what the child has done as writing. Whatever the child does at the start of the unit will change, however, with the amount and nature of writing becoming visibly more advanced as the unit progresses, reflecting all that the children are learning.

Prior to the start of the unit, you may want to set up an experience outside the writing workshop in which children rely on a procedural text to get something done: to make a friendship bracelet, to make play dough. You could follow a procedural text to do that activity, helping children be able to draw on a vivid sense of the genre once they are invited to write their own how-to texts.

At the start of the bend titled "Writing How-To Books, Step by Step" you'll tell children that writers not only use writing to tell stories, but they also use writing to teach others how to do stuff. Instead of proceeding to teach your children the characteristics of how-to writing, you'll simply show them a how-to text, laying it alongside a narrative text, and you'll then challenge your kindergartners to study the differences between story writing and a how-to text on their own, figuring out for themselves how the two genres are different. They'll have no trouble seeing that how-to writers teach others the steps for doing things, and they'll probably notice some other things as well: the steps are numbered, there are drawings for each step. You will then surprise kids by saying, "So right now, go and write your very own how-to book."

That is, the unit starts with you inviting kids to engage in problem solving—What distinguishes this genre from the sorts of writing you have been doing?—and then to do the work, as best they can. You don't assume they'll have tons of trouble and break their writing into tiny steps and coax them along each step, keeping them on a tight leash. Instead, you say, "Go to it," and then you study what your children do.

Of course, children will be writing about things they know how to do, and this means they'll bring their areas of expertise into your classroom. You will discover the hidden talents of your young writers as they write books on everything from "How to Make an Ice Cream Sundae" to "How to Change a Diaper" to "How to Hit a Homerun," to "How to Do Yoga."

Engagement and volume will be high in this bend, because you'll encourage children to choose any activity they know how to do, no matter how big or small, and to give it their best try. Then, too, you will give children room to grow by encouraging them to write one how-to text after another. Become accustomed to asking questions such as, "So is this your first book for today's writing workshop or your second?" and "How many how-to books have you written today?" What you will not want to see is a child who thinks that recording a quick, underdeveloped five-step how-to text constitutes his full work for a day! Along the way, there will be lessons on drawing and writing one step at a time and writing with enough clarity and detail that others can follow the directions. Writing partners will play an important role in this bend as children pair up to test out their directions to make sure everything makes sense and to get ideas from one another. At this point in the year, children are adept at working together with their writing partners. This unit highlights the importance of writing partners and provides ample opportunity for children to "participate in collaborative conversations" with their writing partners, following "agreed-upon rules for discussion" (CCSS SL.K.1.a) and to "continue a conversation through multiple exchanges" (CCSS SL K.1.b).

In the second bend, lessons focus on studying mentor texts and trying out techniques the students notice in those texts. Children will study elaboration techniques, for example, including the fact that how-to writers often tuck tips into their teaching, and they often write directly to readers, using the "you" voice. Many how-to texts use comparisons to make their points clear, and you will highlight that as well. Ultimately, you'll want to use this bend to help your young writers understand that they can always look to real, published books as exemplars and then use what they learn from those texts both to help them write better first drafts and also to go back and revise their prior writing.

In Bend III you will help your children find opportunities across the school day to write how-to books that can be helpful to others. You'll help your children realize that topics are really everywhere and that there are many opportunities in the course of a day for them to teach readers how to do something. In this bend, children will also be encouraged to write a series or collections of how-to books. The books children write will be put into the hands of their classmates, so this bend also includes an emphasis on writing easy-to-read books that actually convey to readers what they need to know.

In Bend IV, "Giving How-To Books as Gifts," you will help your children get ready to share their work, making sure it will reach and help the intended audiences. You will teach writers to think strategically about where in the world their books should go. The book "How to Give a Dog a Bath" might be suited for the neighborhood pet store. The book "How to Make Guacamole" might be important for a restaurant in town. As you work through this book, you'll see also that it sets the groundwork for children not only meeting the grade level standards for writing, but exceeding them.

ASSESSMENT

The improvement that you will see in children's writing will be more dramatic over the course of kindergarten than in any other grade. By the end of this unit, you will find it very satisfying to say, "This is what this child's writing was like at the start of the unit, and look, *this* is what he (or she) can do now!"

Children, too, will find that satisfying, and it is a very big deal to help children see themselves as progressing along a sky-high growth curve.

Of course, you won't be able to remark on the growth that your children make unless you establish baseline data. That is a big reason why we recommended you take a bit of time at the start of the year, and again at the start of the unit, to assess your children's abilities to write information texts. That is, whether or not you've already given children an on-demand writing task in information writing at the very start of the year, you'll probably want to give one just prior to embarking on this unit. This will help you pinpoint the most current needs of your writers.

As you will have learned from previous units, we recommend you use one consistent prompt across classrooms, and even across grades, so that you and your colleagues can gather together to analyze student writing across the board—writing that was created under similar conditions with the same directions. Just before your unit begins, you can prompt a piece of information writing by saying this to your children the day before the assessment:

> "Think of a topic that you've studied or that you know a lot about. Tomorrow, you will have forty-five minutes to write an informational (or all-about) text that teaches others interesting and important information and ideas about that topic. If you want to find and use information from a book or another outside source to help you with this writing, you may bring that with you tomorrow. Please keep in mind that you'll have only forty-five minutes to complete this. You will have only this one period, so you'll need to plan, draft, revise, and edit in one sitting. Write in a way that shows all that you know about information writing."

As mentioned in previous units, you can find this prompt and some additional instructions in *Writing Pathways: Performance Assessments and Learning Progressions, K–5.*

You can make this on-demand writing feel celebratory by saying that you realized by listening to your kindergartners talk to one another that many of them know a lot about so many topics, and you want to give them all a chance to show off even before you teach them anything about this new unit. If you do decide to adapt this prompt in any way—for example, if you decide to leave out mention of bringing in outside books or sources of information—we encourage you to plan this in conjunction with your grade-level team to ensure that you gather consistent data that you can compare across the grade.

The next day, repeat the relevant parts of the prompt, and give the children forty-five minutes to plan and write. Be sure the children are sitting at their usual writing workshop spots and that they have their writing workshop booklets of paper (described below in the Getting Ready section). It is crucial to allow the children to work on their own and to problem-solve with this. Resist the urge to help them! This work will establish a baseline and will likely show what you already suspect—that your children have a lot to learn about informational writing. You might wince at the way the prompt seems to confuse some of your children, but because the plan is to take the work that your children do and merge it with work first- and second-graders do; and, for example, because second-graders' work will be merged with third- and fourth-graders' work, it ends up being important to keep the prompt the same for children at different grade levels. The truth is that your kindergarten children will hear the parts of this that they understand, and the rest will fall by the wayside. Although the prompt may seem confusing, we've actually seen amazing results from kindergartners.

As you move about the room during the on-demand assessment, you won't be surprised if a large number of your children are drawing or writing something that misses the mark. They haven't learned anything about this type of writing yet, and you can expect that this will show, of course. However, you might be surprised at what some of your children *do* do. For example, you might discover that, unprompted, most of your class tends to draw very detailed drawings, complete with labels. This will allow you to customize your unit—spending less time teaching into drawing and labeling so that you can move on to other things. On the other hand, you might find that a large number of children in your class have a tendency to rush through the drawings or rely heavily on copying words from around the classroom instead of making their own best attempt at spelling words. All of this information will be valuable as you set forth in this unit.

One thing that sets kindergarten apart from other grades is that often children's pictures and writing hold meaning but are difficult to read because they are just barely learning to use letters to represent words. During the on-demand assessment you'll need to circulate around to each of your children to get dictations of the writing that you cannot read. You'll ask each child whose writing you can't read to read his or her writing to you, or tell you what the pages say, and on a separate sheet of paper or a Post-it® you'll record what the child intends the writing to say. This will allow you to decipher the meaning behind the pictures and the developmental spelling. This is also a time for you to carefully observe your children at work. For example you will want to check to see that children know how to hold a pen or pencil with a three-finger grip (rather than a fist), and you'll note habits such as putting the pencil down between every letter or tracing over everything multiple times before moving on. Later during the unit, you might decide to gather small groups of children to address these habits to help them learn to write more fluently.

Once the students have done this, you will also want to assess where each writer falls on the Information Writing Learning Progression in the *Writing Pathways: Performance Assessments and Learning Progressions, K–5* book and to note where the bulk of your class falls, letting that assessment inform the upcoming unit of study. To do this, we suggest you read each student's work, comparing it to the benchmark texts, and then read the specific descriptors to hone in on the specific ways that a student can improve. No text will match a checklist in its entirety, so don't be thrown off if a piece of writing, for example, seems to fall somewhere between the kindergarten and first-grade levels. The descriptors will be particularly useful as you help writers know specific steps they can take to make their writing better. That is, if a writer's text is mostly kindergarten level, you and that writer can look at the descriptors of, say, structure, for grade 1. You might have a conversation with the writer, using the two checklists, saying, "You used to have a last page in your writing, like this," and read the corresponding descriptors from the Grade K Information Writing Rubric, "but now you are ready to write an even better ending or conclusion for your work," referring to the Grade 1 descriptor. You might even share an example with the child, citing a section of the grade 1 benchmark text.

We encourage you to duplicate the children's on-demand writing and to place one copy in each student's writing folder, where it can serve as a reminder to the writer and to you that this is the level of work that he or she was able to do at the very start of the unit. The fanfare around the performance assessment probably led each student to do his or her best work when writing the on-demand, so there is no guarantee that subsequent writing will be equally strong. By keeping the on-demand writing close on hand, you can help writers hold themselves to the job of making sure all their subsequent writing *is* progressively better. As students create pieces of writing to add to their folders in the days ahead, ask them to look back frequently at their on-demand pieces, making sure that they are getting palpably stronger in comparison.

After your students publish their final pieces of writing for this unit, you will once again ask them to compose an on-demand piece of writing. The second on-demand will serve as a summative assessment, measuring growth across the unit. Are students writing with greater detail and incorporating strategies to include more details? Is the piece more structured, starting with a clear statement of the topic and ending with a concluding thought or sentence? Are students now meeting or exceeding grade-level expectations?

In addition to the on-demand assessment, you will also want to review your assessments of letter-sound identification and high-frequency words to inform your instruction on the language and foundational standards. You might also administer a spelling assessment if you haven't done so recently. By this time in the year, your students' knowledge about these should have grown in leaps and bounds, and you will want to keep helping them make the link between writing workshop and what they know about letters and sounds, high-frequency words, and spelling patterns.

During the unit, you should also rely on your formative assessments, such as your conferences and small-group work, as data-in-hand. Use this information to assess that students are on track and to teach into the things they are not yet grasping in order to support their progress.

GETTING READY

Before you invite kids to write how-to texts, you will want to prepare paper that can scaffold their writing so that it follows the conventions of this genre. We recommend booklets of five pages, each containing a large box for drawing detailed diagrams and lines for writing. Some teachers prefer to provide a blank space for numbering each page to help children see that this paper is for a new kind of writing—writing that has numbered steps. Be sure the paper you use provides enough room for students to write with detail.

For some children, the best way to support rigor will be for them to write more than one how-to text in a day, but for others the best way to support rigor will be to channel them toward writing more elaborate texts. It will be important for you to talk up the paper choice with more lines—perhaps three or four lines for writing on instead of two or three, with extra single pages available to encourage writers to add yet more pages if needed. In instances when procedural texts span many pages, usually each page represents a single step explained in detail.

The second decision that you need to make is to decide which how-to texts you will use as read-alouds prior to beginning the unit to familiarize the children with the genre. The world is filled with "procedural" writing—cookbooks, instructions for new toys and games, craft projects to make, and so on. You'll want to gather examples of how-to writing so that even before the unit begins, you can start immersing children in the sounds of these texts. Choose a few to read aloud and to study, examining how writers use their words and pictures to teach readers. There are lots of great procedural books; if you want a few to look at for starters, you could look at the "How to Carve a Pumpkin" page in *The Pumpkin Book* by Gail Gibbons or at the books *How to Make a Bird Feeder* by Liyala Tuckfield (Rigby Literacy), or *How to Make Salsa* by Jamie Lucero, *Make a Valentine* by Dale Gordon, or *How to Make a Hot Dog* by Joy Cowley. *Walk On!* by Marla Frazee is a more sophisticated mentor text for children who have written several how-to books with ease and want to take their writing up a notch. Although you will gather many of these texts, you'll also be looking for one or two that can function as mentor texts. You'll return to those texts often throughout the unit. *My First Soccer Game* by Alyssa Capucilli is one that you will see used throughout the unit. You will want to make sure that what children are learning can be transferred to any book and is not specific to one particular book.

To help children grasp what it means to write a how-to text, you might create an opportunity outside the writing workshop to immerse them in the genre—doing or making something with your children so that you can, as you proceed to do that thing together, jointly construct a shared/interactive how-to text. For example, if your school has had a fire drill, you might want to create a how-to chart listing the steps that were involved in that fire drill.

Writers Study the Kind of Writing They Plan to Make

IN THIS SESSION, you'll teach students that before a writer writes, he thinks "What kind of thing am I making?" and then studies examples of whatever it is he wants to make.

GETTING READY

✔ Ribbon and scissors, for a ribbon-cutting ceremony (with an upbeat musical selection in the background) (see Connection)

✔ Pictures of a variety of dogs large enough to be seen by children when sitting in the meeting area (see Teaching)

✔ Previously created "true story" (make multiple copies, enough for one per table) and "How to Turn a Word into a Snap Word" class texts from the *Writing for Readers* unit (see Teaching and Active Engagement)

✔ A simple narrative (see Active Engagement)

✔ A child's how-to book from your collection from past years, from a student from another class, or your own child-version how-to book (see Active Engagement)

✔ Basket of how-to books, one basket for each table. The basket can be labeled "How-To Books" and can include published texts as well as children's writing.

✔ Two types of prestapled how-to booklets for children to choose from on a tray at each table. You may want to offer booklets of three pages and five pages, with 3–4 or 6–7 lines for writing, along with extra pages that children can add on (see Link).

✔ A familiar how-to text that you have read with your class several times before beginning this unit of study and a copy of a page from it. This session uses an excerpt from *My First Soccer Game* by Alyssa Satin Capucilli (see Share).

✔ "How-To Writing" chart that you will create during the share.

✔ Chart paper and markers

COMMON CORE STATE STANDARDS: W.K.2, W.K.5, W.K.8, RI.K.1, RI.K.6, RI.K.9, RI.1.6, RI.1.9, SL.K.1, SL.K.2, SL.K.3, L.K.1, L.K.2

DO YOU REMEMBER HOW EXCITING IT WAS, when you were little, to start a new school year? I loved the new school supplies—the pencil case, the erasers that always smelled so good, even that transparent green protractor that never seemed to have a purpose. I remember flipping through the pages of the clean new notebooks ready to be written upon. For me, the start of the year was always a time for new resolutions, for a new identity. "This year," I'd tell myself, "*This year*, I'll record all my assignments in my assignment pad. I'll write in cursive. I'll write a page a day." Underneath any particular resolve was the fervent hope that I could draw a line in the sand and start on a new and better chapter.

The new unit that starts today can become an especially big deal for your children—a whole new chapter in their writing lives—because they will be making a different kind of writing from anything they have ever made before. Whereas during the first two units they wrote stories, they now turn a new leaf and embark on how-to writing. You can also call it *procedural writing* or *functional writing* or *explanatory writing*. The Common Core State Standards cluster this kind of writing under the larger category of informational writing. These standards suggest that one third of children's time across all subjects and across the entire year be devoted to informational writing. So the work that children embark on today will be important. Eventually they will transfer their skills at how-to writing into math, as they detail how they solve a problem, and to science, as they write lab reports that are a variation of this kind of writing.

This session creates a drumroll, then, around the fact that this is new work. Children are taught that when writers approach a piece of writing, they need to think, "What kind of writing is this?" and "How does this kind of writing go?" The fact that a writer pauses to establish the genre in which he is writing may seem obvious to you, but it is not obvious to children. Think, for example, of the fact that children will soon write all-about books, also called *information books*, which will present its own sorts of demands. By the time children are in first grade, all-about books contain different kinds of writing, with a dog book perhaps containing one chapter on kinds of dogs, one on the day I got my dog, and one a how-to text such as "How to Give Your Dog a Bath." If a child pauses at the start of each chapter to ask, "What kind of text am I making?" and realizes that "The Day I Got My Dog" is a narrative and that "How to Give Your Dog a Bath" is a how-to text, each following different conventions, that will be an important feat! That work is still a stretch for most of your students, but it is helpful to teach with an awareness of what lies beyond the immediate future.

"The fact that a writer pauses to establish the genre in which he is writing may seem obvious to you, but it is not obvious to children."

You will see that this session makes no attempt to teach the characteristics of how-to writing in any explicit way. Instead, children are taught that writers study the kind of text they intend to make, noting whatever they can about that text, and then write accordingly. You leave it up to children to inquire into the characteristics of the genre and to discern that this writing is written in tiny numbered steps, that each step is accompanied by a drawing that serves to teach, and so forth. Some of your children will glean these conventions from their review of finished how-to texts; others may not (in which case you can eventually teach this more explicitly). Either way, they will thrive in your confidence and learn from your implicit message that it is a pleasure to work hard, with independence, on a big job—and that writing contains lots of those big jobs.

Writers Study the Kind of Writing They Plan to Make

CONNECTION

Create a ribbon-cutting ceremony, complete with a song and a proclamation, producing a drumroll around the transition to this new kind of writing.

When the children arrived in the class, they noticed a big red plastic ribbon, preventing anyone from coming to the meeting area. I said nothing about this.

While children were still in their seats, I said, "Writers, this morning I need to tell you that whenever people have built a new bridge or a new library or a new sports stadium, the people organize a ribbon-cutting ceremony for opening day. Before anyone enters the new bridge or library or sports stadium, all the people gather for a ribbon-cutting ceremony. Today we start not only a new unit of study—which is a big deal—but also we start writing a whole new kind of writing! So will all of you gather at the edge of our meeting area for our ceremony?"

Once the children were standing alongside the ribbon, I suggested we sing a writing song—a variation of "If You're Happy and You Know It, Clap Your Hands." I suggested that for our first verse, we sing, "If you're a writer and you know it, clap your hands." Then "If you're a speller," and finally, "If you're a storyteller." Once the song was completed, I took hold of the largest shears I could find, and in a mayoral, commanding voice proclaimed, "Today marks the start of a new unit. As of today, our class will begin a whole new kind of writing." Then we snipped the ribbon, and I announced, "Let the new work begin!" and children thronged to their places.

❖ **Name the teaching point.**

"Writers, today I want to teach you that just like there are different kinds of dogs, there are different kinds of writing. Before a writer writes, the writer thinks, 'What kind of thing am I making?'"

> ◆ COACHING

You may alter partnerships for this unit, in which case you'll need a system for conveying the new alliances to children. Partner talkative kids with quieter kids, kids who ask good questions with kids who tend to be vague, English language learners with language models. In some cases you might find triads work well, putting two children who can carry on proficiently together with a third child who can benefit from the modeling.

TEACHING

Point out that there are different kinds of writing, illustrating this with enlarged versions of a familiar narrative and how-to text, suggesting children ascertain the differences.

"What are these?" I asked, holding up pictures of dramatically different dogs. The kids agreed they were dogs, and some called out the specific breeds. I nodded. "You are right. These are all dogs, but they look really different, don't they? That's because they are different kinds of dogs.

"Let me show you something else." I revealed the familiar class story about the bee that came into our class from the previous *Writing for Readers* unit of study that the class had helped to write and, alongside it, the directions we used earlier in the year for how writers turn a word into a snap word. "These are both pieces of writing, but they are different kinds of writing. One is a true story of one small moment, and one is how-to writing, or you could call it *directions*. Starting today, we're going to be making how-to books." I gestured to the paper showing directions.

"Before writing, the writer thinks, 'What kind of thing am I making?' and then studies examples of whatever he or she wants to make to learn how to do this new kind of writing.

"Today I thought maybe, just maybe, you could do that work all on your own. Do you think that if I read this how-to writing to you and afterward I zip up my mouth and say *nothing*, you could turn your brain on really, really high and see if *you* can study this new kind of writing and figure out how it goes, how it is different from a story, and then do some of this writing all by yourself?"

The children were game. "This means I am not going to tell you anything about how this new kind of writing goes. I'm just going to read you some examples. I know you can do this. I'll read, and then you'll go to your writing place and make your own how-to book, all by yourself.

They agreed.

Encourage students to choose a topic—something they will teach others to do—before channeling children to study the differences between narratives and how-to texts and to get started writing the latter.

"Before you study how this kind of writing goes, you probably want to have a topic in mind that you will write about today. So think of something you know how to do that you could teach others. Like do you know how to braid hair, or to ride a scooter, or to give a dog a bath, or to make pancakes, or to make a goal?" I left a tiny pool of silence. "You have something in your mind? Thumbs up if you have thought of something you know how to do.

"Okay. What are you planning to teach people to do?" I asked and called on just a few children. "Are you ready to study how this kind of writing goes?"

As children become more experienced writers, they may come to know narrative writing as simply "small moments," due to the emphasis over time on writing focused, detailed narratives. Depending on how your last unit unfolded, it may or may not make sense to begin referring to small moments now. In any case you will want to remind students what they already know about narrative writing.

By rattling off examples of very common, everyday things that students are experts at, we are modeling the kinds of topic choices that are available. Students don't have to dig deep to find interesting topics; the things they do every day are enough.

ACTIVE ENGAGEMENT

Abstaining from citing differences, read a narrative and then two different how-to books. Channel children to discuss what they notice.

I read part of a quick narrative and then shifted to read the "How to Turn a Word into a Snap Word" chart (children were familiar with this from *Writing for Readers*), touching the numbers alongside the steps in a significant ("notice this") fashion.

Then, signaling "Wait," I brought out the work a child had done and read his writing.

LINK

Reiterate that writers think, "What kind of thing am I making?" and encourage children to help each other study what goes into a how-to book and then write one as best they can.

My lips still sealed, I gestured for the children to get going. On each table, there was an example of how-to writing and some blank books. Once the children were at their tables, I said, "You can help each other figure out how this new kind of writing goes and get going writing your own."

You can use the "How to Turn a Word into a Snap Word" class text from Writing for Readers, *or you may decide to choose any how-to text that you have written previously. With your class, try to choose a text where the directions have been written with one step on each page, with detailed diagrams or pictures that teach and other features of how-to writing.*

FIG. 1–1   Stapling paper like this into three-page or five-page booklets gives children quick access to the materials they need. You can observe your students at work to determine how many lines per page and how many pages per booklet to offer. Remember to teach kids to select paper that will leave an extra line or two left over, room to add more later.

Welcoming Approximations, Inviting Children into the New Work

Today's CONFERRING AND SMALL-GROUP WORK will be a special pleasure because your main goal will be to rally kids' energy for the exciting new work of this unit. Give yourself a talking-to before you head out around the room. Repeat over and over to yourself, "I will not fuss over whether their work is perfect. I will celebrate approximation. I will celebrate approximation." Plan on enjoying all their mess-ups, for now. If they totally don't get how to write how-to texts, that is absolutely fine. That's why you will be teaching this unit! Imagine how impressive it will be later when you contrast their start of the unit work—today's writing and their on-demand pieces—with their end of the unit work.

So plan to travel quickly among the writers, using table compliments to sprinkle good will and confidence and excitement among them. Pull up to one table where some kids are working. You may note that a few seem oblivious to the fact that this is a new genre, with different conventions. Their writing will look exactly like it looked a week ago. Let that go, for now. Meanwhile, notice that one child is looking at—even just glancing at—the finished how-to book that you left on the table. "Oh my goodness. You all are making such wise decisions—the way you keep on studying the example and keep on noticing the ways that a how-to book is so, so different than storybooks! I am thinking and hoping that if I go to another table and then come back to this one, by then maybe some of you will be talking together while pointing to specific things you notice in your how-to book. Maybe then you can see if any one of you has already done some of the same things that you notice in your own how-to writing! I love the way you know that writers study examples of the kind of writing they want to write and then make their writing the same!"

You may want to carry some Post-its®, or better yet, Post-it flags, with you so that you can encourage children to study and notice features of published how-to texts. It will probably take some doing for you to channel children to notice things such as the format and conventions of the writing, rather than the specific content and information. The child might notice that the author of the washing your dog how-to text does

MID-WORKSHOP TEACHING
Help Children Carry On with Independence

"Writers, can I stop you for a moment?" I waited until their eyes were on me. "I just want to remind you that as soon as you finish one how-to book, you can reread it to make sure it makes sense and then start another one! Don't wait! I see a few of you sitting, waiting. I think you are ready to start a new how-to book! Do it! Get another how-to booklet! You are on a roll. Don't stop now! Go get some paper. You know what to do!"

As Students Continue Working . . .

"In a few minutes we're going to be all out of time. Can you believe it? When I know that my writing time is almost over, I always like to do one last check to make sure that my writing makes sense, sounds right, and looks right. Right now, everybody, reread one page of your writing and ask yourself, 'Does that make sense?'" Then, noticing some writers had yet to start rereading, I said, firmly, "That's right, everybody, right now."

As children worked, I noticed that some of them were rereading their writing, but they had already put away their pens. I said, "Don't forget, you can keep your pen in your hand while you reread so you can revise your writing if you need to. Don't forget, you can use one end of the pen to read and the other end of the pen for writing!"

"Don't forget to point under each word. Check the pictures you drew. Make sure the words match what is in the pictures. If it doesn't match, change it!"

the job indoors and may wonder why she doesn't use a hose out of doors, and that sort of observation won't exactly help the youngster as she writes her how-to book on braiding hair. You may or may not address this disconnect today. There will be other ways to get at this. For children who have no trouble noticing that how-to writing uses different forms and conventions, you may want to point out that noticing what the author has done is one thing; noticing *how* and speculating *why* are even more challenging and important kinds of intellectual work.

Of course, it is one thing for you to allow kids to approximate within this genre and another for you to allow kids to sit frozen over their paper. You are not apt to find that many children struggle over topic choice, but if a few do, you will need to help them get started. One way to do this is to gather those students around the class "Flow of the Day" chart, telling them that this chart, this daily schedule, can always be a secret source of topics they could teach others. Point to the first thing on the chart. If it says, for example, "Morning Meeting," you can say to children, "I bet you could each write a 'How to Have a Morning Meeting' book, couldn't you? Think, 'What is the first step to having a morning meeting?'" After recalling a few steps that could be included in a book about the first item in the "Flow of the Day" chart, you could progress to the second item on the chart, doing the same work with it. "You could each write a 'How to Have Reading Workshop' book, right? What would be the first step in a reading workshop?"

If you were doing this work with a small group of children, you could then say, "Right now, pick one part of our schedule and give me a thumbs up when you've picked one. Excellent. Now turn to the person next to you and take turns telling your first step. 'Step 1 . . .'" As kids begin to name the steps for the event they chose, coach into this work. After they have named the second step, they should probably get started sketching and writing.

As you can imagine, it helps to carry ideas like that one in your mental pocket, so that when you observe children and decide on ways to teach them, you don't need to invent all your teaching on the spot but can draw on a repertoire of ideas for conferences and small groups. For this reason, it helps to talk with colleagues about some of the things they find themselves teaching kids during the actual workshop. If you and your colleagues share and collect ideas for conferences and small groups that will be especially helpful now, at the start of this unit, notice that those ideas will often be transferable to other units as well. For example, at the start of this unit and every unit, you can powerfully use conferences and small-group time to remind children to bring all they know from previous units into this unit. That is incredibly important instruction that has the potential to make a huge difference. (Think, for example, about whether or not, today, kids are touching and telling, using the word wall, rereading often, and so on, and think how helpful all of that skill work will be to this unit.)

Step 1: *Open your drawer. And get your underwear.*

Step 2: *Open your drawer and get your shirt.*

Step 3: *Open your drawer and get your jeans.*

Step 4: *Open the top drawer again and get your socks.*

Step 5: *Get dressed!*

FIG. 1–2   On the first day of the unit, many students will be excited to choose topics they know well from their own experience, and will write an entire booklet in one sitting, like this student did on "How to Get Dressed." Then, in subsequent days, they can go back and add more to each page.

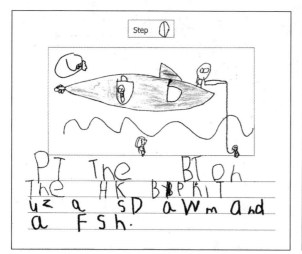

Step 1: Put the bait on the hook by pinching it.
Use a sardine, a worm, and a fish.

Step 2: Next cast the line.

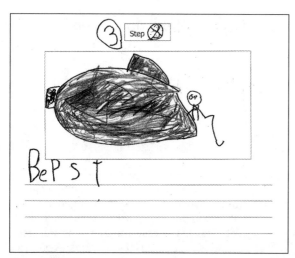

Step 3: Be patient.

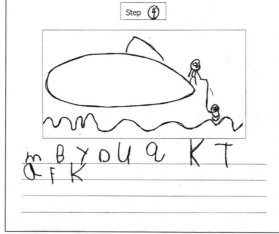

Step 4: Maybe you will catch a fish.

FIG. 1–3   Encourage children to listen for whatever sounds they can hear in a word and to use their alphabet charts and other resources around the room to write words as best they can. There may be students recording mostly initial and ending consonants (like this student, who wrote "How to Go Fishing") right alongside students who spell mostly conventionally.

Compare How-To Writing with Familiar True Stories and Notice Differences

Collect and list a few especially important differences between narrative and how-to writing.

After convening children in the meeting area, I said, "Will someone tell me a way that how-to writing is different than story writing?" As children offered up something about how-to writing, I began a list on chart paper, titled "How-To Writing." "How-to books have numbers!" exclaimed one student. Using a big marker, I wrote, "Numbers the steps." Soon we'd made this chart, listing some key features of the genre.

How-To Writing

1. Tells what to do, in steps.

2. Numbers the steps.

3. Has a picture for each step.

"As we learn more about how-to writing, we will talk more about how writers go about making books like this to teach people how to do many things."

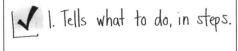

How-To Writing

✓ 1. Tells what to do, in steps.

✓ 2. Numbers the steps.

✓ 3. Has a picture for each step.

Charts are more memorable and meaningful for kids when you create them together. Often you can simply write the chart along with kids. In this case, the chart was prepared ahead of time, minus the checkmarks on Post-its. Then the Post-its were added as the children discussed each item. Notice that the chart leaves room to add more.

Writers Use What They Already Know

Touching and Telling the Steps across the Pages

YESTERDAY YOUR EMPHASIS was on the fact that writers think, "What kind of thing am I making?" and realize that just as there are different kinds of dogs, there are also different kinds of writing. You invited youngsters to look hard at a piece of writing, thinking, "How does this piece of writing go?" and you channeled them to study examples of how-to writing to identify features of the new genre. Some of them will have done this successfully, and some will need your help. Today you provide that help in a way that suggests you are merely compiling all that they noticed from their careful study.

As you do this, remember the advice from Stephen Covey: first things first. Your goal is not to deluge children with an overwhelmingly large inventory of every conceivable trait of procedural writing. So this means you will not want to ask repeatedly, "What else do you notice that authors of how-to writing do? What else? What else?" For example, writers of how-to books often include little warnings or cautionary notes. There is no reason to mention this now, and in fact doing so takes the wind out of a later minilesson.

You can collect answers from children while still shaping the eventual list by asking children to turn and talk about their observations, eavesdropping, and then calling on children whose observations are especially foundational. You can also add more observations to the list you collect. "Did some of you also notice that . . . ?" you can say, and then articulate whatever you wish your children had contributed.

As you talk about the characteristics of how-to writing, you'll weave in examples of this writing, helping to prime the pump so that children generate topics they will write about today. Some children may not have finished yesterday's how-to book and may need to return to it, but in general, your expectation can be that children will write at least one of these books each day. Whereas many will start the unit off by writing a few words for each step in the process, before long you'll be expecting closer to two or three sentences for each step.

IN THIS SESSION, you'll teach students that writers draw on what they already know about planning, touching, and telling the steps of their how-to books across pages.

GETTING READY

✔ Booklets (with extra pages that children can add on) in a tray on each table. On each page, there will be a box for children to number the steps.

✔ Children will come to the meeting area with their writing folders today (see Connection).

✔ "How-To Writing" anchor chart, created in Session 1 (see Connection and Share)

✔ How-to writing piece from a student, either one that you have saved from a previous year or from a student in another class or Cooper Loval's piece on the CD (see Connection and Share)

✔ Students' writing from the previous session (see Connection)

✔ Enlarged version of the booklets the children are using for shared writing. You can prepare half sheets of chart paper with a box for sketching and lines for writing to look just like the paper the children use (see Teaching).

✔ Idea for a class how-to book that you and the children will begin making during today's teaching and active engagement.

COMMON CORE STATE STANDARDS: W.K.2, W.K.5, W.1.2, RI.K.1, SL.K.1, SL.K.4, SL.K.5, L.K.1.e,f; L.K.2

Writers Use What They Already Know

Touching and Telling the Steps across the Pages

CONNECTION

Today, call children to the meeting area with writing folders in hand. If this is new to your class, ask the children to sit on top of their folders to reduce distraction. Remind children of the list they made about how-to writing, and then read another piece and ask them to check whether it matches those descriptors.

"Writers, remember at the end of yesterday's writing workshop, when we studied *My First Soccer Game*, you made a chart listing what you noticed about how-to writing?

"I'm going to read a piece of writing that a writer in another class wrote, and I want you and your partner to notice whether this piece of how-to writing has all these things." I reread the chart.

"Ready?" I held up a book, reading the cover title: "How to Play Kickball." "The author of this book is Cooper Loval." Then, turning pages, I read:

Step 1—Make sure you make the teams.

Step 2—When the ball comes, kick it. If someone catches your ball you're OUT! But if no one catches your ball you're safe!

Step 3—When it is three outs go in the field to catch a ball.

Step 4—If you catch a ball the other person is out!

Step 5—Good catch. Thanks.

(See Figure 2–1.)

(See Figure 2–1.)

◆ COACHING

Anchor charts are meant to be referred to again and again. They should become an active teaching tool and not merely decoration for the walls of your classroom.

How-To Writing

1. Tells what to do, in steps.

2. Numbers the steps.

3. Has a picture for each step.

You can substitute a different example of how-to writing here, if you wish. It is helpful to find examples on topics that are familiar to the children, making it easier for them to understand the content.

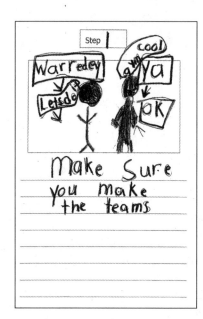

Step 1

Make sure you make the teams

Step 2

Wen the Ball coms kick it if some one Ball your catchis your Out! But if no wun catchis your ball your Safe!

Step 3

Wen it is three outs go in the feld to catchch a ball

Step 4

if you catch a ball the ather pus in is Out!

Step 5

good catch thanks

FIG. 2–1 Cooper writes his steps across pages, numbering each step, and includes a picture for each step. He also does more, including warnings, dialogue bubbles, and sentence variety. For now, you don't need to highlight everything—save some for later in the unit.

"Did this tell what to do, in steps? Thumbs up or thumbs down. Did Cooper number the steps? Did he include a picture for each step?" The children agreed he had done these things.

Ask children to contrast the book *they* wrote the previous day to the list of descriptors, encouraging them to revise today so their book fits the bill as a how-to book.

"Right now, please look at the book *you* wrote yesterday, and see if you already did the things on our chart, or if those are things you are going to do today." I gave them time to do this.

"Can I see thumbs up for how many of you *already* put the first step, then the next, then the next in your first how-to book?" Many children gestured thumbs up that they had done this already. "Today you can fix up or finish yesterday's book and write a new how-to book! Who knows what you will teach people to do today? Tell each other your ideas."

After a moment of buzz, I said, "Terrific. If I take your books home tonight, I'll learn how to make brownies and to play basketball and to ride a scooter and to make a friend! I'm going to have a busy night!"

❖ **Name the teaching point.**

"Today I want to teach you that when you write a how-to book, there are *new* things to do," and I gestured to the how-to chart, "but it also helps to use some of the *old* techniques you *already* learned when you were writing stories. You *still* say what you are going to write across the pages—touch and tell—and you *still* draw the pictures, saying the words that go with a picture. Only this time, each picture and page is another step."

TEACHING

While writing a class text, demonstrate how to make a how-to text, first coming up with a topic, then saying each step while touching one page at a time, and then sketching.

"Let's write a how-to book together, about something we all know how to do, so that we can practice touching and telling with how-to writing, because before now we only did that with stories. I was thinking that all of us know how to have a fire drill, because we had one just the other day. So let's get out how-to paper and remember that we first touch and tell, only this time we are telling what to do, in steps. Watch how I touch and tell the first steps of a fire drill, and then you can touch and tell the next steps."

I put my hand on my chin and pondered for a moment. "I better first remember how the fire drill goes." I looked up in the air, pulling a memory from the sky, and then, as I recalled the sequence silently to myself, I registered each step on another finger. I took hold of an enlarged chart paper booklet, touched the first page and wrote-in-the-air "How to Have a Fire Drill." Then I touched the next page and said, "Step 1. When the bells ring, it is time for a fire drill." Moving to the next page, I said, "Step 2. Then you get your jacket and get in line."

This connection is highly engaging: rather than simply looking at a text, children are asked to be active by giving a thumbs-up and by talking briefly with a partner. These added levels of scaffolding are helpful when children need extra support with new or challenging information.

Sharing and mentioning a variety of kinds of how-to books helps. If you only highlight how-to books about sports, then you are more likely to see only sports books, and the same holds for other topics.

It's helpful to use expression in your voice, as well as gestures, to emphasize the language, "Step 1 . . . step 2 . . ." Putting the emphasis on this language will help your children hear and understand that this type of writing is different than writing a narrative.

Debrief. Name what you just did as a writer.

"Writers, did you see how I named the first steps in the fire drill, just touching the page and telling what I would write on that page? I used touch and tell, just like we used that strategy for true stories about small moments."

ACTIVE ENGAGEMENT

Invite writers to add the last couple of steps to the class how-to book, writing-in-the-air on imaginary booklets.

"Writers, it's your turn now to try doing the same for a few of the steps. Can you tell your partner what could be the next steps that you can add to our 'How to Have a Fire Drill' book? Partner 1, pretend you are holding a booklet, and turn the pages back to the very, very start of your imaginary booklet." I waited. "Are you on the title page? Starting with the title, tell all the steps, including the ones we just said, and then keep going, past where I stopped. Do all the steps 'til you get to the class standing outside, okay? Partner 1, hold your imaginary booklet, point to the cover, and start!"

As I approached Sofia, she was saying to Preston, "Step 4. You walk outside and line up across the street."

To the whole class, I said, "Once you've touched and told up to the part where the class is outside, pass the imaginary booklet to your partner and let Partner 2 give the steps for coming back inside."

Preston pretended to touch the page and said, "Next, listen for the whistle and come back in the school." I moved quickly to listen in to other partnerships.

LINK

Remind writers that after rehearsing the entire booklet, they go back to page 1, sketch, and write.

"Writers, when you are writing, after you touch and tell the pages, you will want to go back to page one and touch that page, say the words to yourself, and then draw the picture for that step. Remember, as you draw the picture, it helps to say in your mind what you will write!"

I wrote "1" in the box at the top of the first page and then quickly made a sketch for the first step, saying the words as I did this, and then quickly wrote the words.

"Writers, we all just worked together on 'How to Have a Fire Drill,' but does that mean you all have to write a how-to book about fire drills? No! Of course not! You can write a book that teaches people to do anything you know how to do. Thumbs up if you have your idea for what you will teach in today's how-to book." The children signaled. "Thumbs up if you are ready to touch and tell your own how-to book across the pages?" Again, most signaled yes. "Fantastic. There are new booklets waiting for you in baskets at each of your tables. Some of you may still need to finish yesterday's book, so do that first. As soon as you get back to your writing spot, you can get started! Off you go."

Imaginary booklets are quick and ready to go, with no additional materials for children to manage at the meeting area. (Remember, they are already sitting on their writing folders.) An alternative would be to provide blank booklets, as a more tactile way to practice today's work.

Varying Small-Group Methods and Structures

YOU SAY TO THE KIDS, "Off you go!" and of course, it's not only the kids who get started. You do as well. For a moment, you'll want to just watch as they make their way from the meeting area to their work places. Be mindful that this is a moment for you to do some important assessment. By this point in the year, all your children should be able to make the transition from the meeting area to their writing places, from listening to writing, without needing an intervention. If they seem to need you to run from one child to another, giving individual jump starts, that's a problem.

So watch them get started, and if you see that there are many in the classroom who have become so dependent on you that they just sit at their writing spots, waiting for you to get to them and say, "What are you going to write?" and then, "Great, put that down," then you'll want to decide on some actions to take to support greater independence. That action can provide more or less scaffolding. The least scaffolded response would be a voiceover, delivered to the whole class as children work (or don't work, as the case may be). "Writers, I should see all of you rereading what you wrote yesterday and then either finishing that book or starting on a new one." Another way to nudge writers to get started is to move quickly among the children, using nonverbal cues to signal, "Get started." A tap on one child's page, a gesture that says, "Get writing" delivered to another, a firm "Now" to a third.

If children need yet more help, you might try table conferences. Pull up a chair alongside a table full of writers, and be sure they do not stop to talk to you but instead continue their work. "Just ignore me and get going. I want to study the way you work," you can say, holding your clipboard at the ready. If few actually are working, then you probably want a small-group conversation. "Writers, I'm confused. Why aren't you writing?" The conversation may need to become a little lesson on getting yourself started in your writing.

Once all your writers are writing, you'll be able to decide what to do. It can help to quickly consider your options. Do you want to confer individually or lead small groups? If you feel that many kids are needing some help, choose the latter. Then you can think,

---

MID-WORKSHOP TEACHING **Writers Need Not Sound Out Every Word; Some Words They Know in a Snap**

"Writers, I love seeing that some of you are remembering that you don't need to stretch out every word. Some words you just know in a snap. Like, let's say you want to write that when the fire drill bell rings, you stand *in* line. Right now, with your finger-pen, write *in* on your hand.

"How many of you said, '*In*. I know *in*,' and you just wrote it? Good for you. And did some of you say, '*In*. That's on our word wall,' and glance up at the word wall? Good for you! As you keep working, I know you'll be stretching some words out. And other words, you'll know in a snap!"

As Students Continue Working . . .

"Don't forget to reread your writing, and ask yourself, 'Will someone else be able to read this?'"

"Writers, I love all the different how-to books I am seeing. Listen to some of them: 'How to Set the Table,' 'How to Play Laser Tag,' 'How to Ice Skate,' 'How to Make Hot Chocolate.' And there are many more. Can you believe how many things we will be able to do after we read each other's how-to books?"

"Can I tell you about a problem that Jennifer solved by working hard at it? She is writing a book about how to be a good friend. She didn't have enough paper for her steps, so she went to the writing center, got two more sheets of paper, took apart her booklet, added in more paper, wrote her two more steps, and then stapled her book back together! Good problem-solving work, right?"

"What are four or five possible topics I could teach in small groups?" Or you can think, "What are several possible methods I could use to lead small groups?"

Let's say you decide to go with some different methods. You should have a bunch of these at your fingertips. For example, one method for teaching a small group is to confer with one child and then gather a group of kids together to say, "Can I show you what so-and-so just did that some of the rest of you might try?" Then you need to story-tell the sequential story of what you helped the one child to do, only we generally take ourselves out of that story so that instead of saying, "Then I told her to reread her writing," say, "Then she decided she'd reread her writing."

A second method for leading small groups revolves around the use of a mentor text. You can convene a group of writers and say, "One of the things that I do a lot as a writer, and I know most writers do, is that I study examples of the kind of writing I'm trying to make. So I thought maybe the group of us could study this how-to book, and you guys could try to figure out some things *you* could do to make your books really, really special."

Another way of leading small groups may involve treating these as essentially peer-response groups. You could gather several partnerships and set children up to alternate reading their writing aloud and giving each other feedback. If you decide to do so, you could channel children to give feedback on specific things, such as on each other's teaching pictures or on the clarity of the directions. You could, over time, work with children so that they anticipate that when you listen to their small group or partner conversations, you'll use gestures to signal ways they can improve the conversations. You can teach them that whenever you point to the paper, this is meant as a signal for them to reference the writing more exactly. When you point to a person other than the speaker, this is a signal to let that other person join into the conversation. Children, of course, will enjoy helping you devise signals for all that you might want to say to a small group, and in doing so, they rehearse ways to improve their conversations.

Then, too, small groups can be designed as inquiry groups, with writers bringing their work to the group and expecting to lay their work out and study what they have done and what others have done. When doing this, students can look across the work that several children did, identifying an instance where one writer did one thing or another especially well, and they can talk about what made that work exemplary. Of course, the natural next step is for children to help each other emulate the successful model.

Checking Writing against the Anchor Chart

Remind writers that earlier they had looked at student writing to see ways it aligned to the list of characteristics of how-to writing. Do this again, with the day's new writing.

"Writers, earlier today we looked at Cooper's book to see whether it had all the characteristics of the how-to writing we studied. Look at the new writing you did today, and see if it matches all that we have observed about how-to writing. As I read each item from our chart, will you and your partner point to places in your writing where you did that item from our chart? And if you haven't *yet* done some of this, you can work together to do it now." I then read from this list, pausing between each item."

The share is an opportunity to deepen the work that children have done so far. Yes, nearly all your children will be drawing and/or writing steps by now. But with how much detail? And did they reread their work to make sure it all makes sense? You can adapt this share session to highlight work that your particular students will benefit from.

> ## How-To Writing
>
> 1. Tells what to do, in steps.
>
> 2. Numbers the steps.
>
> 3. Has a picture for each step.

As children reread their how-to books to check for each item on the chart, I stood up from my chair to read over their shoulders. I made a short list of things that I noticed could use improving. Once we'd moved through all three items on the chart, I said:

"You are really thinking like writers now, rereading your own work! Now, I noticed that almost everybody had steps and numbers, and almost everybody had pictures for each step, BUT I also noticed that sometimes the pictures didn't really show much action. For example, look at Cooper Loval's book again. See how the people in his pictures are just standing there? You can't really tell what they are doing, can you? I think it would help a lot if every picture actually showed what the people were doing, don't you? Writers, right now, will you add to one of your pictures to make sure that really shows exactly what is happening? Try moving the arms or legs, add objects if you need to, or draw where the person is. You should probably use labels, too, to help us learn from your pictures."

Writers Become Readers, Asking, "Can I Follow This?"

THINK FOR A MOMENT about the way you learn skills, for example, the skills you have been learning about teaching writing as you work through these books. Presumably, when you started the first few sessions of the first book, you taught a full writing workshop. You gathered children, gave them a minilesson, sent them off to write, worked with individuals and small groups, and then convened the children. Now you continue to do all those things, but thinking about writing instruction is much more nuanced. You are aware of the differences between minilessons in which you use your writing as an example and those in which you rely on a child's piece of writing. You are aware that sometimes a minilesson ends with children getting started writing while they are still on the rug, and sometimes you send children off to work on their writing. And so on.

"This minilesson is the cornerstone of the unit. Prepare yourself to have a lot of fun, to let your children collapse into giggles."

In the same way, children will have been using fundamental skills repeatedly. For example, a month or so ago, at the start of the *Writing for Readers* unit, children learned that writers reread. They learned that writers use one end of the pencil to write, then flip the pencil over and use the other end of the pencil as a pointer to help with reading. Today you return to the concept that writers reread, only this time, your focus is less on the word work of rereading one's own writing and more on the work of comprehension and monitoring for sense, and you will teach the specific ways writers reread how-to writing.

This is a favorite minilesson. It was a mainstay in the first edition of Units of Study for Primary Writing. In many ways, it is the cornerstone of this unit. Enjoy it. Prepare yourself to have a lot of fun, to let your children collapse into giggles.

IN THIS SESSION, you'll teach students that writers reread their writing as they go, making changes along the way.

GETTING READY

- ✔ An example of student writing, displayed for the class to see (see Connection)

- ✔ Students' writing folders, from the previous session, and pencils (see Connection)

- ✔ An example of student how-to writing whose steps are unclear or difficult to follow (see Teaching)

- ✔ Chart paper and markers for rewriting part of a how-to booklet (see Active Engagement)

- ✔ Successful (easy to follow) how-to writing by one child in the class that he or she will read during the share

- ✔ "How-To Writing" anchor chart from previous sessions on display

COMMON CORE STATE STANDARDS: W.K.2, W.K.5, RI.K.1, RI.K.2, RFS.K.1, RFS.K.2, SL.K.1, SL.K.2, SL.K.3, SL.K.6, L.K.1, L.K.2

SESSION 3: WRITERS BECOME READERS, ASKING, "CAN I FOLLOW THIS?"

19

Writers Become Readers, Asking, "Can I Follow This?"

CONNECTION

Celebrate one child who reread her how-to book, reminding all students of the importance of rereading.

"Writers, yesterday I saw Sofia writing her how-to book, and do you know what she did? She wrote one of her steps, and then after she wrote that step, that page, she flipped her magic pencil over to the other end and used it as a pointer to help her reread her writing.

"Sofia, I've got your book displayed on the easel. Can you come up and show the class how you reread your writing?" Sofia scrambled up to the front of the meeting area and used her pencil's eraser to tap out her words. (See Figure 3–1 on p. 21.)

> Step 1–First take the cover and pull up. Make sure you hold with two hands.
>
> Step 2–Then you smooth it out to make it smoother.
>
> Step 3–Next take the blanket and pull it up with two hands.
>
> Step 4–Then put the pillow up with two hands. Stuff it up.
>
> Step 5–Put the stuffed animal on.

"Writers, you see how Sofia crossed words out and added in more words? What happened is that she reread her book and realized, 'Hey, wait a minute. I could say more!' Then she added the missing parts. That's good work, Sofia, to remember what you learned earlier about writers needing to become readers and about revision. You remembered that work from when you were working on your true stories last month!"

Bring home the importance of rereading by asking students to reread their writing from the day before, making small revisions as they go.

"Right now, will each of you get out the books you wrote yesterday? Use the eraser end of your pencils to reread just a page of your books, for now, and then if something is missing, do like Sofia did, and flip your pencils back to the writing end and fix things up."

You may have noticed that in minilessons where students will use a piece of their own writing, we usually ask them to bring their entire writing folder to the meeting area, even when only one booklet is needed. Many teachers find that a consistent routine for bringing work to the meeting area helps to move things along and avoids confusion. Alternatively, you could direct children to bring one how-to booklet instead of the entire folder.

There are many different ways you can have students share their writing during a minilesson. Sometimes it is enough for a student to just read her writing aloud. However, in this instance, it was important that the rest of the class actually see Sofia's writing, as well as the way she used her eraser to tap out the words as she read. Pages can be pulled apart and displayed side by side. Or if you have a document camera, simply use that to enlarge the writing.

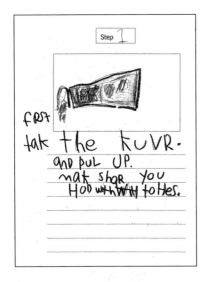

Step 1

fRST
tak the kUVR.
and puL UP.
mat shoR you
Hod with wht to Hes.

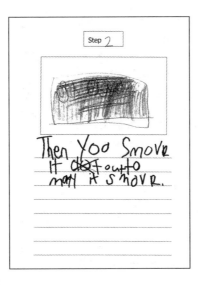

Step 2

Then Yoo Smovr
it daf out to
maty it s novr.

Step 3

Next tau
the bLuRt ann
pLit UP. wit to Has.
wihto Has.

Step 4

then
Staff it up.
is put the piow
up with to Has.
st uf it u p

FIG. 3–1   Sofia revises her book on how to make a bed by simply crossing out the parts she'd like to change.

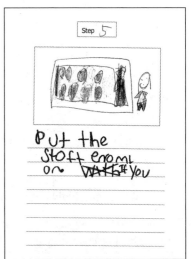

Step 5

Put the
stoff enome
on wakf it you

For a moment, children worked. I signaled that those who finished before the others could move on to their second pages.

✤ **Name the teaching point.**

"Today I want to teach you that how-to writers don't just reread the words, touching them with a finger or a pencil. How-to writers *also* reread to check that their writing makes sense. To do that kind of rereading, writers reread to a partner or to themselves and make sure it is easy to follow the steps."

TEACHING

Demonstrate what it means to check your directions with a partner, noticing whether the directions make sense or need to be revised for clarity.

"The best way to check whether your directions will make sense is to read them to someone who will try to follow the steps, to do whatever you are teaching (for real or for pretend). If the partner can't figure out what you mean, if he or she can't figure out what to do, that means your directions don't *quite* work, and then you can revise them.

"Let's try reading the words of one of your books and see if we can follow those words, okay? Sam is writing a how-to book on doing a somersault. He'll read it to me, and let's all see if I can follow his directions." I brought Sam to sit on a chair beside my chair.

SESSION 3: WRITERS BECOME READERS, ASKING, "CAN I FOLLOW THIS?"

21

"Sam will read me his book (just the start—it isn't done), and I'll do whatever his book tells me to do. Writers, when you do this kind of reading—when you read directions—instead of reading the book straight through, it helps to read one step and then do that step, then read the next step, and then do that step."

Sam read, "First put your head down and your legs up." I looked at him, as if asking *"What?"* He reread, "First put your head down," and, still sitting on a chair at the front of the meeting area, I tucked my chin toward my chest. Then Sam read, "And your legs up." (Remember, I was still on the chair!) "Okay, my head is down, but hmm, my legs go up? To somersault?" I raised my feet so they stuck straight out from the chair. A bit puzzled, I said, "Okay, keep reading."

Sam had by now covered his eyes in dismay, though we could all see his huge grin. He read his next page, starting to giggle: "Then turn over."

"Turn over? I'll hurt myself!"

When the writer of confusing directions makes verbal revisions, capitalize on this, and name that, yes, after checking for clarity, writers often revise.

Sam started to protest that when he had told me to put my head down, he meant I needed to put my head *on the floor* and that of course I needed to get off the chair to do so, but I returned to the role of teacher rather than gymnast to be. "Are you saying, Sam, that now you realize you need to make revisions to your directions?" When he nodded vigorously, I said, "That's what happens when you reread your writing to a partner and see the way that person struggles to follow what you have written."

ACTIVE ENGAGEMENT

Ask children to think with their partners about ways to revise the original instructions. Attempt to follow the revised instructions, highlighting the idea that being specific makes directions easier to follow.

"Tell your partner how you might start a book on doing somersaults that could maybe work better," I said, and the room erupted into conversation.

Convening the class, I called, "Okay, let's try out another set of directions for doing a somersault. Just tell me the new steps, and I'll follow them."

This time the first step was "Sit on the floor."

"Okay, first you sit on the floor." After I clamored off the chair, I wrote on a piece of chart paper, "1. First, sit on the floor." "Okay, I've done that. What's next?"

"Put your head on the floor." I touched my face to the floor, not putting my head in the proper position.

Another child called, "No! Put the *top* of your head . . ."

I pointed out, "That's a smart revision! Put *the top of your head* on the floor." On the chart paper, I wrote, "2. Put the top of your head on the floor."

"You are getting better at realizing the details your readers will need. We'll stop here for now. This is such smart work! You are thinking about your readers and writing steps that will help them."

LINK

Tell children they'll need to decide what they will do, knowing many will recruit a partner to help them reread to check that the partner can follow the text.

"Writers, writing time is really your work time. Today as you work, think about everything you have learned so far." I gestured to our anchor chart to remind children of some of the key points. "You can be the boss of writing time and decide what you need to do to be sure you have a whole folder full of great how-to writing. Let's just think about what you *could* decide to do today. Who has an idea of what you could do?"

Sam suggested, "I could write an *even better* book on somersaults and headstands too 'cause I know how to do them."

I nodded, agreeing that writers could write whole new books. "And if you do that, write the directions so I won't fall and break my head, okay? So you might write whole new books. What else might you do today?"

One writer piped in with "Reread?" I practically fell off my chair over the brilliance of her suggestion. "You aren't going to need a teacher anymore. You are learning to teach yourselves. How totally cool that you take the stuff we did with Sam's book and imagine doing it with your own books. Do you mean you might bring your book to someone in the class and say, 'Will you try to do what I say?' and then watch whether they get as confused as I did?" The children nodded vigorously.

"Might you even *revise* your book to make it clearer? That would be *so* grown-up." The kids were definite that they'd absolutely do that.

"Oh my goodness. So get going. Don't waste a second. I gotta see this."

SESSION 3: WRITERS BECOME READERS, ASKING, "CAN I FOLLOW THIS?"

23

Anticipating that Some Children Will Need Scaffolds and Supports to Access High-Level Work

THE MOST PRESSING THING YOU WILL NOTICE TODAY is that some children will quite rightly tell you they can't follow each other's directions. "I can't ski in this room, can I?" they'll say. You will need to show children that they can read each other's directions and *imagine* following them. If the directions say, "Break an egg on the edge of the bowl," the reader can grasp an imaginary egg and break it on the edge of the imaginary bowl. If the directions say, "When the person in line in front of you gets on the ski lift, push yourself forward quickly so that you are standing in the place where the lift will get you," then perhaps the actor is a finger puppet made from your two fingers, who pushes forward on imaginary skis. The important thing to realize is that the process of reading directions is a stop and go activity. The reader reads a step, then does the step—really doing it or imagining doing it. Then the reader presses on, reading the next step. This sort of reading can be done in a way that reveals potential problems in a draft.

While children read their how-to writing to each other and work to address the problems they see, you will want to also read their writing and think about how you can address the problems *you* see. Whereas the kids will address problems by adding words to their pages, you'll address problems with small-group work, mid-workshop teaching points, and minilessons you write on your own to address issues that we never imagined.

For example, if you find that your children are choosing topics such as "when I went to my grandma's house" that don't set them up to write procedural pieces, then you will want to spend more time immersing them in the sounds of procedural writing. This means it will be important for you to read how-to writing aloud. Don't talk this reading to death. Just read and immerse your children in the language of the genre. Meanwhile, find opportunities to give the class oral directions. "Today we're going to make bracelets. Let me teach you how. Listen. I'm going to give you all the how-to directions now. You'll see my directions will be like a how-to book. First, you . . ." Meanwhile, help children develop lists of topics that match the genre and key phrases they can use at the start of these texts that help to angle their writing. For example, you might have these words, hanging prominently in your classroom: "Do you want to know how to . . . ? I will teach you. First you . . ."

> **MID-WORKSHOP TEACHING   Writers Say It a Different Way if a Partner Doesn't Understand**
>
> Near the end of writing time, I spoke up loudly, getting the children's attention. "Writers," I said, "eyes on me. When you read the directions from your how-to book to your partner, and your partner says, 'Wait, I'm confused. I can't follow these directions,' that's your signal that you have to do something. Do you just leave it the way it is and go on? No! Of course not. Here's a tip: try saying it a different way, and then ask your partner, 'Does it make sense now?' Then take your pen and cross out the old writing and put in the new way of saying whatever was confusing."

It may be that in your class there are one or two children that need extra special help getting started. Perhaps these are children who are just learning to speak English, or perhaps these are children who are extremely reluctant to take risks for fear of getting it wrong. In any case, the heaviest scaffolding you could provide might be to offer up the class how-to book to these few individuals to write as their own. You might say, "Remember how we wrote 'How to Have a Fire Drill' together yesterday? Well, guess what? The kids who come to this school next year are not going to know how to have a fire drill, and it would be great to have that written as a book. Would you each be willing to write that book for them? You could help each other." By offering each child a blank booklet and encouraging them to say those familiar fire drill steps aloud, you're helping them transfer familiar language and vocabulary from one context (whole-class, shared writing) to another (on their own in a small booklet). Encourage them to put it in their own words and draw their own pictures now that they have their own small booklet to write "How to Have a Fire Drill." As soon as they are up and running, leave them to continue, not without letting them know that they can write their next how-to book on any topic they choose!

Envisioning the Steps in a How-To Book and Revising if They Don't Make Sense

Ask children to join you in listening and mentally following one child's directions.

"Today I saw something really terrific. Listen to this. I saw many of you reading directions not only to your partner, *but also to yourselves!* You reread what you wrote and thought, 'If I follow my own directions, will they work?' I have asked Nicole to read her how-to book to us. As she reads, let's close our eyes and see if we can picture ourselves doing each of these steps."

Nicole read her writing.

> Nicole
>
> How to Plant a Flower
>
> 1. First dig a hole. Then put the seeds in the hole.
>
> 2. Cover the hole with dirt. Water your flowers.
>
> 3. Then give your flower some sunlight and take care of your flower.
>
> 4. Talk to your flower. Then your flower will grow.

Nicole hadn't yet finished the book, but she told her classmates what she planned to write on the final page: "One day it will start to grow." "Thumbs up if you were able to see the steps of that happening." Thumbs went up across the room. "I feel ready to plant a flower right now!"

Ask children to turn to their partners and read aloud. The listener will try to imagine doing the steps.

"Writers, would you get with your partners? Partner 1, read your book to Partner 2, just like Nicole read her book to us. And Partner 1, listen and see if you can picture yourself doing each step. Are the directions clear? Do you know what to do first and next and next?"

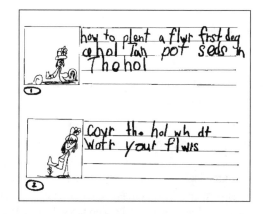

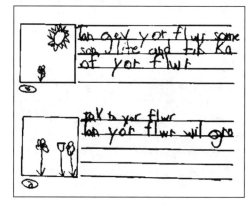

FIG. 3–2   Nicole's writing is easy to follow, in part because she writes more than one sentence for each step. This simple strategy could be tucked into small-group, conferring, or even a mid-workshop teaching point or share.

I listened in as Troyquon turned to his partner, Rachel, and began to read:

A Cook Book How to Make Pizza

Step One: Throw up the dough.

Step Two: Spin the dough in your fingers.

Stept Three: Pat the dough into a flat circle.
            Put tomatoes onto the dough.

Step Four: Put tomatoes onto the dough.
           Put the dough into the pan.

Rachel interrupted after Troyquon read Step Three. "A flat circle? How will it look like a pizza, not a donut?"

Help writers realize that if listeners aren't able to follow the steps in a how-to book, revision is necessary.

I agreed. "Rachel is asking a good question. That's so helpful, isn't it Troyquon? With that help, you can go back and reread and think, 'Have I told her enough?'"

Troyquon looked dubious about reconsidering his text, and it was time for the share session to end. Seizing the moment, I said, "I'll tell you what—why don't I take your directions home and try following them. I'd love to eat some pizza tonight!"

Troyquon took a sticky note and carefully wrote his telephone number. "If you need me, call me."

I convened the class. "Class, I'm going to follow Troyquon's pizza recipe tonight. I have a Post-it with his phone number in case it doesn't work. Will you listen and tell me if you think I'll need to call him?" I read Troyquon's piece to the class. "Thumbs up if you think I'll need to call him." Most of the kids raised their thumbs. "Hmm. Well, I'll give it a try and let all of you know tomorrow if I get stuck!" I made a mental note to follow up with this during morning meeting the next day.

FIG. 3–3 Troyquon's pictures are nearly as helpful as the words for readers to understand his directions.

Writers Answer a Partner's Questions

TRY WRITING IN A WAY that allows someone else to learn from you. You'll find it is not easy! Certainly you have found times when this book is not as clear as you wish it were. "Huh?" you ask. "What are you saying?"

It is especially challenging for a five- or six-year-old to write clear directions for someone else because children at this age are egocentric. They tend to see the world through their own eyes and not imagine that others see something different. It was but a few years ago when these children were toddlers who would cover their eyes up and say, "You can't see me." They'd be standing in full view in front of us, but because their eyes were covered and they couldn't see us, they assumed that in fact *they* were invisible!

It is a very big deal, then, to ask children to write in ways that take into account what others need to know to fully comprehend a message. The words of your minilesson won't be enough to make children able to imagine another person's perspective. Instead, you will want to use your minilesson to channel children to engage in repeated practice, doing the sorts of things that will (after repeated practice) eventually allow them to walk in the shoes of someone else—in this case, a reader.

The great news is that you have the one most important scaffold for this sort of intellectual education right at hand: a partner. The great psychologist Lev Vygotsky had it right when he suggested that learners can first do with the help of someone else what they can eventually do on their own. The goal of today's minilesson, then, is not so much to inform students about a new concept as to create for them another opportunity to experience another person's perspective.

IN THIS SESSION, you'll teach students that writing partners help each other make how-to books clearer and easier to follow.

GETTING READY

✔ An enlarged version of the text used for demonstration in Session 2 ("How to Have a Fire Drill") (see Connection)

✔ A loaf of bread, jars of peanut butter and jelly, a plate, and a plastic knife or spoon (see Teaching)

✔ A book you have written on how to make a peanut butter and jelly sandwich (which you'll pretend to have found on your desk that morning). Include the following steps, deliberately leaving the directions open to misunderstanding) (see Teaching).

1. Get the jar of peanut butter.
2. Put it on the bread.
3. Now get the jelly.

✔ "How-To Writing" anchor chart from previous sessions on display (see Mid-Workshop Teaching)

COMMON CORE STATE STANDARDS: W.K.2, W.K.5, RI.K.1, SL.K.1.a, SL.K.2, SL.K.3, SL.K.6, L.K.1.d, L.K.1, L.K.2

Writers Answer a Partner's Questions

CONNECTION

Once you have a captive audience, reread the class how-to book aloud. This provides a novel way to remind children of relevant prior instruction.

When the children gathered, I made myself busy rereading our class how-to book, "How to Have a Fire Drill." I first flipped my pencil around and used the eraser end to reread, pointing to each word, fixing up a small thing or two as I reread. Then I started to reread a second time, acting out the steps as I read them. Partway through this, I feigned finally noticing that the kids were all waiting for me.

"Oh, so sorry. I didn't notice that you were all here. I was so busy rereading. Readers, I know some of you have been rereading your how-to books too. How many of you have reread them with your magic pencil, touching each word and fixing things up if you see that you left something out?" The children signaled that they had, and I nodded, then added, "How many of you reread your book to someone else, checking to see if they could follow your directions?" Again, many children signaled that they had done that.

❧ **Name the teaching point.**

"Well, today I want to tell you that writers feel really lucky if they have readers who not only try to follow their directions, but who also speak up, saying things like 'I'm confused' or 'Can you explain that more clearly?' when they need to do so."

TEACHING

Remind students that writing partners are wonderful helpers.

"Have you ever noticed that inside many books there is a section where the writer says, 'My thanks go to so-and-so, who helped me with this book.' Some of you are probably going to end up wanting to write one of those thank-you sections inside the cover of some of your books, because your partner is a really good writing helper.

> ◆ COACHING

By modeling for the class how I reread with my magic pencil, making revisions as I go, I am showing them that these habits are a way of life. All writers reread their writing and make revisions. It's not enough for us to simply tell children to do it—we need to show them how we do it, too.

"I've written a book that I want to put in the school library for all the kids to read, but it isn't quite finished yet. I was hoping you could all help me finish it today. I'm going to show you how to be a helper for me, so that you can be great helpers for each other."

Recruit a child to play the role of your writing partner. Coach the child to act out the steps of a how-to book and give suggestions for making it stronger.

"But before I ask for everybody's help, I would really love a partner, a helper, who tries to follow my directions and who also has the courage to tell me (nicely) places where my book is a little confusing. Would one of you be willing to be my writing partner?"

I soon had a partner, Julissa, sitting next to me at the front of the room. "I'll read the book to you. Do you want to follow it in your mind or for real (because my book is one you could do for real)"? My partner shrugged, unclear, so I laid the loaf of bread, jars of peanut butter and jelly, plate, and plastic knife I'd earlier tucked behind my chair before them. "Okay, I'll read my steps, you follow the steps—and tell me if you are ever confused."

Then I said to the rest of the class, "Julissa is my writing partner right now, but all of you can join along. Will you all pretend you have an imaginary loaf of bread, and imaginary jars of peanut butter and jelly in front of you and try following this book too?"

Then I read (hoping to confuse the kids).

> 1. Get the jar of peanut butter.
> 2. Put it on the bread. (I expect kids to put the jar on the loaf.)
> 3. Now get the jelly.

By now, some kids were laughing. I looked startled. "What are you saying? My directions weren't clear enough for you?"

Tell students that writers use their partners' feedback to revise their books for clarity.

The kids let on that the directions were confusing. "What?" I asked. "Julissa, you are my writing partner. You will tell me the truth, right? Does my how-to teach you all the steps? Does it make sense?" Julissa giggled and said, "No, it doesn't. You told us to put the *jar* on the bread!"

I pretended that this was a major realization for me. "Oh, I see. It is confusing. Let me try those directions again, changing them to clear up your confusion."

When we teach people to do something—to swim or to teach or to write procedural texts—one of the challenges is deciding what matters. What skills do we want to be sure learners develop? It'd be easy to teach writers details about the features one finds in how-to texts. The trick is to steer our teaching away from trivial pursuits! Here, we have decided that we want children to grasp the idea that how-to books are written for readers with sequenced, clear directions.

Be sure to choose a topic that is meaningful and familiar to your students. Whether you decide to write "How to Clean a Guinea Pig Cage" or "How to Make Chocolate Pudding," the essence of this lesson is the same.

1

Get the jar of peanut butter.

2

Open it, and using your knife, scoop out a knife-full of peanut butter.

3

Spread the peanut butter over one piece of bread.

My thanks go to my writing partner and my readers, who helped me know parts of my first draft were confusing.

FIG. 4–1   This chart-sized how-to book will become a shared text the class adds to throughout the unit. Using the method of shared writing, the kids will contribute the ideas for the writing, and the teacher will take the role of scribe (though we often restate or add to children's contributions as we go). Thus the shared text that is created is a joint effort, a collaboration between teacher and students.

This time, the kids had more success. I paused. "I'm not going to finish all these directions, but I just have to tell you that tonight, I'm going to add a new section to my book. I'm going to say, 'My thanks go to my writing partner and my readers, who helped me know parts of my first draft that were confusing.' Thanks so much for helping me.

"Writers, did you see how helpful it was to have a partner who was brave and honest with me. She let me know that my writing was confusing and I needed to explain things more clearly, didn't she?"

ACTIVE ENGAGEMENT

Ask students to generate ideas about how to be helpful partners.

Julissa returned to her seat to join the class. "Writers, right now turn to your partner to talk about ways you can be even more helpful to each other."

The room erupted in conversation, and I listened in. Lexi was in the middle of her conversation with Oliver. "You are a good partner when you tell me I left out a word. 'Cause I said 'I poured the into Daisy's bowl,' and I forgot to write 'dog food.'"

Oliver nodded. "*And* tell Daisy is a dog. 'Cause they might think it is your *sister* eating dog food!" The two pantomimed eating yucky dog food, and I noted to myself that at some point I'd tell them that laughing together also makes for a good partnership.

LINK

Remind children that they'll not only get suggestions from partners, but they'll also revise to respond to those suggestions.

"Today when you are with your partner, you can listen closely to your partner's how-to book and really act it out, step by step. When you aren't quite sure what to do to act it out, ask your partner to say more. You could say, 'What do I need to do next?' or 'I'm confused. Can you say more?'

"The important thing will not just be to listen to a partner's questions and confusions, but also to realize that when the partner is confused, that is a signal that you need to revise your book to make it clear. How many of you remember about adding extra pages to a book?" They signaled yes. "How many of you think you could use arrows to squeeze more information into the right spots in your books?" Again, many signaled yes. "You can add sentences, or even whole pages to your how-to book, just like I did when you guys asked me questions!"

Create a drumroll around the upcoming end of this bend in the unit, and rally kids to start new books sometime today.

"Writers, you probably will begin by revising the books you have already written, but then you will definitely start a new book. Pretty soon, we're going to come to the end of this part of our unit, and we're going to celebrate by laying *all* your how-to books out, like in a museum. You are definitely going to want to have a whole bunch finished. So get started, quick as a wink."

If you worry that this will be an invitation to chaos, you can settle for asking writers to read directions to themselves and imagine what their readers will make of each step. But we recommend letting other kids try out the directions.

Conferring with Writing Partners

AS YOU'LL REMEMBER, just as minilessons follow a particular template, so, too, do conferences. At the start of a conference, you will generally want to do some quick research to learn what the writer is working on. That research usually begins with a bit of observation and listening. Of course, the observation and listening is especially easy when a writer is working with a partner, since this externalizes what children are doing and thinking. For example, when I pulled alongside Melissa and her partner, Nicole, I first listened long enough to learn that the girls were trying to figure out how to try out Melissa's directions for making chocolate lollipops. Nicole had a pout on her face, and she threw up her hands with exasperation.

"So, writers, can you fill me in on what you are doing now?" I asked.

Nicole said, "I am supposed to try Melissa's directions, but she doesn't have the chocolate, so I don't know how to do it."

Melissa responded, "I'm reading my writing and Nicole is doing my directions, but she's not doing them."

"*I can't!* I don't have the chocolate!" Nicole explained.

Listening to the two, it was of course immediately apparent to me that they were struggling a bit, but frankly, I was also pleased. It had been a day or two since I'd taught them to try out each other's and their own directions, and these two girls had initiated doing this work on their own. This made it easy to move on to the next stage of a conference, supporting the writers by naming something that they had tried.

"I can see you both are frustrated, but you know what? You are trying to do something really smart—testing out the directions to see if they work. And the really important thing is that even though it was a few days ago when I taught you to do this, you haven't forgotten and haven't needed me to remind you that this is a strategy you can use any day. You're doing it all by yourself."

Then I added what was essentially the teaching point for this conference. "But do you remember how, in the minilesson, I said that sometimes we are going to need to *pretend* that we are following the directions? Writers have to do that a lot. When I wrote about peanut butter and jelly, I had to pretend, so I could get the exact words down."

MID-WORKSHOP TEACHING **Writers Not Only Revise Old Books; They Also Write New Books**

"Writers, I'm glad you have been revising. This classroom has felt like a carpentry shop with kids taping strips of paper into their books and stapling new pages into books. Give yourselves a pat on the back if you have done some revision to make your writing even more clear for your readers.

"Although I am glad you've done some revision, I also want to remind you that you need to get started on another book. A good way to know if you are ready to start another book is to use our chart as a checklist." I pointed to our anchor chart.

How-To Writing

1. Tells what to do, in steps.

2. Numbers the steps.

3. Has a picture for each step.

"If you have done all these things, then chances are, you are probably ready to start another book! For just a second, let's remember all the things that you know how to do that you could teach others. How many of you know how to do something related to sports. Like, maybe you know how to throw a Frisbee, maybe you know how to do a headstand, or maybe you know how to arm wrestle. If you know something related to a sport, you could write about that. All of you know something related to school. You know how to count and how to count by twos and how to add and take away, right? If you have little brothers or sisters, they do not know those things, and you could be their math professor. Or you could write a book teaching some little kid in your life how to read. Give me a thumbs up if you have an idea for a how-to book that you will get started on right this second." The children signaled, and I said, "Fast! We only have fifteen more minutes."

Knowing it was now time to teach, and deciding to teach through guided practice, I said, "Nicole, let's both be readers, and we'll listen to Melissa's directions and *pretend* we're making chocolate lollipops in our minds. Let's see if we can let the words help us create a picture (just like when we read about being at the ocean and create the picture). Let's try together, okay?"

Melissa began, "Melt the chocolate."

"Okay, so Nicole and I are going to pretend now. Nicole, let's do it. I held up my hands as though ready to grab something out of the air, but then stopped. I looked up into space as if trying to conjure up an image. "I'm having a hard time getting a picture in my mind. I can't make a picture of how to melt it. Do you put it in your hands like when you put snow in your hands and it melts?" Then I turned to my coreader and said,

"How about you, Nicole? Do Melissa's words tell you enough to be able to imagine how to do this?"

Nicole said, "No. How does it melt? Do you light a fire?"

"You have to put the chocolate over hot water to melt it," Melissa clarified.

"*Oh!* Now I can picture how you do it! First, you put the chocolate over the hot water and that is how you melt it," I restated the first step in Melissa's directions, adding the new information.

"Melissa, keep reading. Read the next step." As she read it, I said, "Nicole, try to imagine what her words are saying in your mind. Then you can tell Melissa what you see, and she can check whether her directions are doing the job."

Melissa continued, "Put the melted chocolate in the mold."

I looked over at Nicole to see if she seemed to be making a mental picture and asked what she was seeing. She said, "I'm pouring it in. It is spilling all over."

I gave her a thumbs up. Melissa, however, added. "Wait. You have to get a spoon and put the chocolate in the mold slowly with a spoon."

"What a smart revision you just thought of! Later you better put that down!"

By this point, it was time to end the conference, so I did as I generally do at the end of a conference. I quickly debriefed, reminding the girls of the strategy we used to link it to the writing work they would do in the future. "So, Melissa, now you need to go back and reread your first page, trying to make a movie in your mind of it—'Melt the chocolate'—and see if you can remember what you need to do differently on that first page so that readers will be able to make a movie in their minds of the whole thing. Then reread the next page, and so on."

Getting the Most Out of Extended Writing Time

Cancel the share so there is more writing time, and rally kids to write fast and furious. Do this in ways that make a statement about the need to produce new writing often.

"Writers, we spent so much time helping each other and revising today that many of you haven't yet gotten very far in your new books. We wouldn't want today to go by without tons of writing, so let's work right past the share, to the very end of writing time. That gives you five more precious minutes for writing, so work fast as a bunny, and see how much you can get done in five minutes. Then, after five more minutes, we'll show each other how much we wrote today. You ready? On your mark, get set, go!"

As children wrote, I called out some voiceovers:

"Just because you are writing fast, you won't want to skip the details that really help people know what you mean."

"If you are writing just one sentence for each step, push yourself to say more, to add at least one more sentence to each step."

After children wrote, fast and furious, for five minutes, I said, "Wow! You all wrote so much! Show each other what you accomplished, and let's hear you complimenting each other. I should hear you saying things like, 'Great job. You really worked hard!'"

Step 1:
First 2 sups X Go In
the DOg Bl !

Step 1: *First 2 cups go in the dog bowl!*

Step 2:
Fll the Athr
Bl With wotr

Step 2: *Fill the other bowl with water.*

Step 3:
Put the
Bls On the Matt

Step 3: *Put the bowls on the mat.*

Step 4:
Cal Hovr ovr
to Et

Step 4: *Call her over to eat.*

FIG. 4–2 Encourage children to make pictures that teach the most important information, as this student has done.

Writers Label Their Diagrams to Teach Even More Information

IN THIS SESSION, you'll teach students that writers add detailed information to their writing by labeling their diagrams.

GETTING READY

✔ Class shared writing on how to make a peanut butter and jelly sandwich with diagram added, covered with sheet of paper (see Teaching)

✔ Kids come to the carpet today with a marker or pen and a large Post-it stuck to a hard writing surface such as a clipboard or white board (see Active Engagement).

✔ "How-To Writing" anchor chart on display in the classroom (see Link)

✔ A volunteer in the class who will act as a teacher, using expressions, gestures, and pointing to teach the class how to follow the steps in his or her how-to book.

"WASSAT?" ASKS THE TODDLER, pointing at a tree.

"That's a tree," we say patiently.

"Wassat?" she asks, now pointing at the clouds. "Wassat?" Now pointing at the grandmother walking her dog. "Wassat? Wassat? Wassat?"

We all love a label. Even as we grow older, we look for language to pair with images. We may step in close to read the plate below a painting in a museum, looking for the artist's name, the date, and the title so that we can think more about what we see. Or we may part the leaves in a flat of annuals to read the little plastic spear, stuck into the dirt, that names the flower and tells us how much sun it needs and when to plant it. In books, we seek out the captions under photos, the labels on cross sections and graphs. No matter our age or experience, we all use labels to give shape and add meaning to images.

Today we invite children to help shape the meaning others take in when looking at the images they have created; we invite them to write labels.

In some ways this is a very basic session. The work seems supportive and uncomplicated. Once children have made an image, they need only point at some part of it and a word or phrase will come to their mind, and they will know what to write. On the other hand, this work is not as simple as it seems. To write a label very well, a person needs to think carefully about what the reader needs to know—and also what he doesn't need to know. Too much information is confusing!

Today's session, then, taps into our human need to put words to pictures, and yet it also nudges children to think about audience and to think about each detail's relative importance in a how-to text. These are not simple challenges, though every child will be able to find a successful way to handle them.

Our world is not a simple place with simple labels for things. This session is meant to move children farther along the path to learning that, while still setting them up to enjoy the concrete fun of drawing pictures and arrows and messing with sticky notes.

COMMON CORE STATE STANDARDS: W.K.2, W.K.5, RI.K.7, RFS.K.1.b; RFS.K.3.a,b; RFS.1.3.a,b,d,e; SL.K.1, SL.K.5, L.K.1, L.K.2.c,d; L.K.6

Writers Label Their Diagrams to Teach Even More Information

CONNECTION

Remind the class of the preceding day's problematic effort to follow your less-than-ideal directions, and point out that you learned you needed to add more detail.

"Remember the other day when the first draft of the peanut butter and jelly book said, 'Put the peanut butter on the bread?'" I acted this out again, with the jar balanced on the loaf. "That book didn't work at all, did it? I had to go back and write the book with more detail, so it said, 'Using a knife, scoop out a knife-sized lump of peanut butter.'

"What I learned from your help is that details really matter. Our book did a better job once we added details like 'open the peanut butter,' 'put the knife into it.' Right?"

❖ **Name the teaching point.**

"Today I want to teach you that one way that writers add detail to information books is by adding detailed pictures called *diagrams*. Writers often help readers understand their how-to books by making detailed diagrams and by labeling the diagrams, using the most precise, specific words they can."

TEACHING

Show that you have added detail to the preceding day's directions by adding a giant diagram, but without labels. Recruit children to join you in thinking about how this is different than illustrations in a picture book.

I unveiled an enlarged, poster-sized (not-yet-labeled) peanut butter and jelly diagram that I had intentionally kept under wraps until this moment. "Many of you have been asking me, 'What is under that sheet? What is it?'

"This is not just a regular picture of a peanut butter and jelly sandwich. With your partner, please think about how this is an unusual picture, and think about how this can help a writer to include details in her how-to book."

After the children discussed for a minute or two, I stopped the hubbub. "You are right that a diagram has much more detail than a regular picture. It shows all the parts and ingredients very clearly. This particular diagram is missing one thing that might add even more information. Thumbs up if you have an idea. Yes, you guessed it. Labels!"

◆ COACHING

During the connection component of a mini-lesson we often reiterate the content of the previous minilesson before teaching children the new focus of today's work.

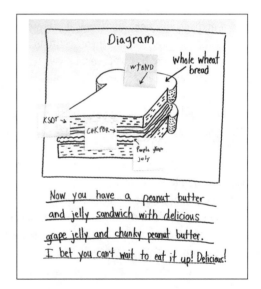

FIG. 5–1 Students and teacher collaborate to create a diagram for their shared writing.

It's fun to think up ways to make your lessons enticing. Whether you cover up the day's materials or put them in a box with a note saying, "Don't peek," you can find playful ways to encourage interest in the day's work.

Demonstrate how to label diagrams, using precise words.

"Watch how I label a few parts of my diagram as clearly and precisely as I can, using the most exact, specific words I can think of. I like to do it like this: first I point to a part. Then I try out saying a few different words and pick the clearest ones. Let's see this part there. That's the bread. The crust. Whole wheat bread, actually. That's it! I'll label it 'whole wheat bread.'" I stretched out the words and wrote them as I said this last part, just tucking in what kids already know about writing trickier words. I added an arrow pointing directly to the bread.

Restate what you've just done, naming each step explicitly.

"Did you see how I did that? First I pointed, then I said a few different words, and then I picked the best, most exact words I could think of to label one part of the diagram."

ACTIVE ENGAGEMENT

Recruit children to help you continue adding more labels to your diagram, prompting them to include specifics.

"All right, now it's your turn to give it a try! Each of you has a Post-it that you can use to make a label for our peanut butter and jelly diagram. Right now, if you are sitting on a red square or a green square, you can make a label for the top part of our class diagram. If you're sitting on a purple square or a blue square, you can make a label for the bottom part of the diagram. This way we will have labels for all the parts of the diagram. Remember, try to pick the very best, most precise words you can think of, words that will really help your reader understand what to do and how."

As I circulated around the carpet, I prompted a few kids to get more precise. "What kind of jelly was it, again?" "Was that crunchy peanut butter or smooth?" "How much jelly did we use? Oh, yeah, I think it was about a tablespoon." "Which label should your reader see first? I mean, which one should get the line all the way to the top of the page?"

As kids began to finish up, I collected a handful to show. "Writers, look up here. I think you are really getting the hang of adding lots of detailed, precise information to your diagrams. Check this out. Vivian wrote 'purple grape jelly' to use as a label right here, and Damien wrote 'chunky peanut butter' to use right here. I'm going to stick these labels on right here and here. I think the peanut butter one should go on the top, so the reader sees it first, and I think an arrow to the right place on the drawing will help too. That way it is *really* specific."

LINK

Before you send children off, remind them that as they revise, finish, or start new books, they can also provide detailed information by labeling their diagrams.

"You already know many ways to make sure your how-to books clearly teach readers how to do something. Remember our chart?" I pointed to the anchor chart that had been on display nearby the meeting area all week long.

It is helpful for young children to point to a part of the picture first and then label that part. The concreteness of touching the actual page makes it all the more explicit and engaging.

As you read this, you may notice that these labels aren't so much labels as they are phrases or captions. This is because we want to emphasize detail and writing information as much as possible in everything the children do in this unit—including the labels. Labeling with more specificity and detail will in turn lead to writing sentences with more detail and specificity.

"Now I think we can add one more thing, can't we? Labels!" I added "has labels that teach" to the list.

"Today you might work on going back over all the books you have written to find places where you might add even clearer, more specific labels. Thumbs up if that's what you plan to do today." Almost every thumb went up. "You might also decide to finish a book you started yesterday. Thumbs up if you'll try that." Half of the kids kept their thumbs up. "It's great that some of you plan to do both of these things! You can use your writing time to do lots of different things—both go back to old pieces that you thought might be done and finish up ones you've just started. And, of course, you'll start new how-to books when you're ready. Remember, when you are writing how-to books, it often helps to label your diagrams with very clear and specific labels that teach the reader lots of information. You can write your labels straight into your book. You may want to use arrows and numbers to make sure your readers know what part of your diagram a label goes with.

"As you leave the meeting area and head to your writing spot, will you add your label to our class book?" I called each table to their writing spots, giving them time to stick their labels onto the peanut butter and jelly how-to book.

FIG. 5–2   Diagrams with labels can be added as a separate page in a how-to book, or they may be incorporated into the steps, as this student has done.

How-To Writing

1. Tells what to do, in steps.

2. Numbers the steps.

3. Has a picture for each step.

4. **Has labels that teach.**

Building Vocabulary and Developing Language

TODAY'S MINILESSON set your class up to be thinking carefully about word choice and vocabulary. It's likely that groups of children in your class will need your support in coming up with the precise, domain-specific words to label their diagrams. "How can my children write labels," you might ask, "if they simply don't know what all the parts are called?"

If you suspect this is the case with a particular child, you might decide to confer into vocabulary with her. Pull up next to her and ask her to say aloud the labels and sentences that will go with her picture. If she cannot, you could coach her by pointing to part of her picture and asking, "Is this a . . . ," naming the part of the object for her. When she says yes, ask her to say it back by simply asking, "What is this?" She'll then name the object for you. "Oh!" you'll say. "This is a . . . ," and you'll name the object again. "Try writing it!" Encourage the child to say the word herself slowly, stretching it out so she can really hear the sounds. "Write the sounds you hear." Of course, having an alphabet strip handy will be helpful.

By this point in the year, you know your children well. It's likely that you have identified a group of children who could benefit from more practice with oral rehearsal of their writing. Some children might say the steps of their own how-to books aloud in ways that sound choppy or disjointed, as though it must have been some other person who wrote the words. In a conference you might ask a child (or a small group of children) to "pretend to write" a page—to tell you aloud exactly what the page will say. The first time the child says a sentence aloud, it comes out choppy. They might be thinking of the words one at a time without putting the meaning of the whole sentence together. Ask them to say the sentence aloud to you again, perhaps with the same details that are included in the pictures, or perhaps with more smoothness. Let them know that saying it aloud again and again until it comes out how they want it is what writers do. Writers practice the way the words go until they like the flow. Ask them to rehearse the sentence even a third time, this time with expression. You might even model saying their sentence with the appropriate emphasis, and even gestures. "From now on," you might end, "try rehearsing your sentences three or four times before you write. That way you can really smooth out what you want to say. *Then*, try writing it."

MID-WORKSHOP TEACHING **Writers Use the Detailed Words in Their Diagrams to Write Sentences that Explain Their Steps**

"Writers, I am learning so much information just from your diagrams in your how-to books! Remember, all of the details in your pictures and labels can also help you to write your sentences. Let me show you what I mean.

"Take a look at our peanut butter and jelly how-to book. Notice all the great details we put into the picture and the labels. Would I just write, 'Look at the thing. Eat it.'? No, of course not! I want to try to use all the details in the picture when I write my sentences. I might write, 'Now you have a peanut butter and jelly sandwich with delicious grape jelly and chunky peanut butter. I bet you can't wait to eat it up! Delicious!' See how the second draft I just said uses the details from our labels?

"I'm going to add that now to our chart." I used a caret to insert the word *detailed* into step 1 on our anchor chart, so that students would be able to see it on the chart and remember this lesson. "Right now, try it. Point to something important in your diagram. Now make sure that you use that information when you write the steps on your page. Ready? Go ahead, get started."

How-To Writing
1. Tells what to do, in _detailed_ steps.

2. Numbers the steps.

3. Has a picture for each step.

4. Has labels that teach.

As Students Continue Working . . .

"I just saw Christian rereading the piece he just finished and starting a new book, just like that! Remember, after you've finished one book, reread and get started on a new one!"

"If you're not sure whether the labels you're adding to your diagrams are clear enough, just ask your writing partner or someone else sitting near you."

"Jarrett just told me about the diagram his mom and dad were studying last night when they were putting together the crib to get ready for his new brother or sister on the way. So cool! Diagrams with labels are everywhere—and they are so helpful, right Jarrett?"

Writers Read Their Writing with Expression

Recruit an expressive reader/writer to read the class his or her how-to text, complete with intonation and gestures.

"Readers, for the share today, I am going to step aside, and William is going to be your teacher!" During conferring time, I'd checked in with William to make sure he was up for this and to have him do a quick practice read. He was delighted! I continued, "But before I go anywhere, I just want you to notice some of the things that William does. I think you can do them, too." I ticked these points off on my fingers as I said them.

"William (one) raises his voice and slows down for the really important things. He also (two) uses hand gestures." I demonstrated the wagging finger, the mini hand-chop, and even the two-hands-over-his-head motion for the really exciting parts, without saying a word and stealing his thunder. "And he (three) points to the pictures that match what he is saying! William, will you come up here and teach us, from your book, how to ride a scooter?"

William came up to the front of the class. "First!" he exclaimed, holding one finger in the air. "You have to put on your helmet." He wagged his finger in the air and pointed to his picture. Then, with a mini-chopping motion for each word, he emphasized, "This. Is. Very. Important."

William continued on as the rest of the class listened, rapt.

"Wow! Writers, did you notice all the hand gestures? The expression? The pointing to pictures? Do you think you could be like William today when you teach your partner from your how-to book? Yes? Good. Turn to your partners now. Partner 2, it is your turn to go first!"

Writers Write as Many Books as They Can

ear Teachers,

Nothing is more consistently helpful for young writers than encouraging more writing. We all know that the more writers practice—with coaching—the more they will grow. That is why coaching your little ones to write more and more *and more* is crucial. Now is the time to focus on that point, since now children have a sense of the form in which they are writing. Now that they have already written several how-to books, they should begin to feel more secure in the genre, so encourage them to produce more books. With each new book, more of the process of writing in this form will become automatic, freeing up their minds for new learning.

You, too, probably have a strong sense by now of the form into which you are teaching. We offer a letter at this point rather than a more detailed description of the teaching we've done so that you have an opportunity, a little friendly nudge, to try your hand at writing (planning) more of your own teaching for this session. What follows are some suggestions for each of the structures of the session. Undoubtedly, you will have your own ideas and budding plans for ways to support children's writing stamina and ways to support them in writing more and more. These are simply our ideas to date for you to use as you see fit—as is all of the curriculum in these units.

MINILESSON

To rally children's attention for concentrating on increasing the volume of their writing, you might offer up a little analogy.

For example, you could tell children about when a friend taught you a dance called the Macarena. Your friend told you the steps to do, and you did one, then the next, slowly, deliberately, plodding your way through the process. And your friend said, "You got it! Now, do it faster, like this," and all of a sudden she was whirling through the dance steps in a way that left you saying, "Huh? What did you just do?"

COMMON CORE STATE STANDARDS: W.K.2, RFS.K.3.c; SL.K.1, L.K.1, L.K.2

So your friend showed you that, in fact, what she had done was just what you now knew how to do—slowly, step by step—but she was putting all the actions together in a way that just flowed along.

You could use that story to say, in your teaching point, that once they know all the steps to writing a how-to book, and they have slowly, carefully written a book or two, they need to learn to do all those steps much more quickly. The best way to learn that is to practice and to push themselves.

For the teaching portion of the minilesson, you need to decide what to teach and how to teach it. In a way, there is not much to teach if your message is just "Write more how-to books, and write them faster! Practice!" So this frees you to think about little tips you could give your students that will help them do just that. You might decide, for example, to teach your children a collection of tips that helps them develop the habit of writing faster, longer, and stronger. Those could include tips for writing with more flow. Writers benefit form saying a whole sentence at a time, then writing that sentence (and a period at the end) without stopping. That works better than saying a word, writing that word, taking a break, and then trying to think of the next word. Then, too, you could give tips for getting more writing done—such as setting a goal. The goal could be a number of lines per page or a number of pages per book or to finish a book in a day.

In addition to thinking about the content of the teaching part of your minilesson, you will want to think about the methods you will use during this portion of your minilesson, You have several methods of teaching to choose from. You could:

- **Demonstrate** a way of writing even more.
- **Set up an inquiry** by asking kids to figure out, with their partners, a way to write even more.
- **Explain** some ways that writers write even more, **and give an example** of someone who has done it.

If you've chosen to demonstrate in your teaching, you might say something like, "Children, one way writers manage to write more is by setting goals for themselves. I'm going to do that right now. Let me look over what I've written and give myself a goal. So far I've written about one line for each of my pages. I'm going to push myself, hmm, maybe double? Yes, I'm going to push myself to write two lines for each page from now on. It will be hard, but not too hard for me. I'm going to write two lines across the bottom of the pages in this new booklet to remind myself to fill them both up with writing, with more detail."

As usual in the active engagement, you'll ask children to try some of what you've demonstrated or described in the teaching portion of the minilesson. You might ask children to turn to their partner and talk over a goal they can give themselves that will help them write even more of their ideas. You might then ask them to plan a way to remind themselves of that goal, perhaps jotting a note or reminder of some kind on their next empty booklet or stack of booklets.

"Children," you might say, "writers are always thinking over ways to write more, to get more of their thinking on to the page, and oftentimes, writers figure out ways to set goals for themselves to help them write more. Throughout your lives, you can always pause to set a goal if you want to push yourself!" Then, as is often the case in the link portion of the minilesson, you might remind children of all the different kinds of work they can do today during the workshop, and of the resources in the room they can use to solve their own writing problems.

CONFERRING AND SMALL-GROUP WORK
Spelling Tricky Words as Best You Can and Moving On

Independent. Resourceful. Creative problem solvers. These are the words your want to be able to use when describing your kindergartners. Not quite there yet? There are a few common issues around independence that are helpful to hold in mind as you head off to confer—today, and every day.

First, it is imperative that children are able to maintain their work long enough for you to pull a student or a small group aside while the rest of the class continues writing on their own. Do you find that when you are working off to the side with just one or a few students, the rest of the class isn't getting very much done? If this is the case, then stamina needs to become your main focus for the whole class before you can resume individual conferring and small-group work. Try coaching the whole class with reminders such as, "Keep that pen in your hand the whole time, even when you are thinking! Don't stop!" or "When you finish one story, put it in your folder, and go straight to the writing center to get another booklet." You might decide to reemphasize drawing and labeling, or you might even introduce new writing utensils for the sheer purpose of enticing children to write. One simple trick is to switch from black pens to blue pens in the spring. Many teachers find that this small change is exciting enough to reinvigorate students. After trying a few of these strategies and reestablishing students' independence during writing time, you can begin to pull small groups and to confer one-on-one with students again.

With the whole class at work, there are bound to be some predictable issues that stump even the most resourceful of young writers. And one of those issues is, of course, spelling. Many of your children have probably begun to use letters and sounds and are beginning to build up a bank of words they know by sight. This means they also can begin to tell when a word is still not spelled correctly—even after they have labored over it, stretching out the sounds to hear them and recording the letters they hear. Some children will go back over the word again and again, reluctant to move on from that word because they know it doesn't look right. You may want to pull together a few children who fit this description to teach a strategy to help them give the word their best try, and most importantly, *move on*, even if the word isn't perfect. You might teach them the "give it a go" strategy: write the word three times on a Post-it to "give it a go" and then pick the one that looks best. A different strategy is to give the tricky word their best try and circle it if they know it still isn't perfect, so that they can ask their partner about it later or come back to it on another day. Whatever strategies you decide to teach, the most important thing is to emphasize that writers problem-solve, all the time, on their own. Independently. Resourcefully. Creatively.

MID-WORKSHOP TEACHING
Keep Your Pen in Your Hand the *Whole* Time!

You might be surprised to discover how many children are in the habit of writing one letter at a time, or only one word at a time, putting their pen down, and looking away from the page after each letter or word. Take a moment to observe your children's writing behaviors. Do they use an appropriate grip? Are they spending time tracing back over letters or words they already wrote? Are they forming letters by pulling down from the top? It's a wise idea to keep these behaviors in your mind, reminding children to practice strong habits that will lead to more writing.

For your mid-workshop teaching you might say, "Writers, I'm noticing that some of you are writing one letter at a time, putting your pen down in between each letter. You'll get a lot more writing done if you keep your pen in your hand the *whole* time. Try it now, everybody. Pick up your pen, like this." Then hold up your own pen, just like theirs. "Put your pen on the paper. Ready, set, start writing. And don't put that pen down." Watch as the children resume writing. If any kids put their pens down, say, "Everybody, even when you're thinking about what to write, think with your pen in your hand." Then you might move around the room using nonverbal gestures to remind kids not to put their pens down.

You might also remind writers of the saying they've heard before—"When you're done, you've just begun!"—to remind them to start a new piece as soon as they've finished.

SHARE

As you near the end of the first bend in the unit, you could use the share time to give children a sense of how well they are doing. You could build up excitement by letting kids know that tomorrow they'll have a very special writing workshop. They'll get to hang up one of their how-to books anywhere they want. You could take a few minutes today to show kids how to pick a piece to revise for your mini-publishing. As always, you will want to emphasize that writers choose pieces that they really love to revise and publish. "Right now, could all of you look in your writing folder to pick out just one special how-to book? Pick one that you would like to work on even more. We will have time tomorrow to revise these and make them even better." You might have kids mark their chosen piece with a special star-shaped Post-it or a special sticker, so that tomorrow, they'll already have one piece picked out.

Perhaps you'll take the share time today to pose a question to the kids. "Where could we display our how-to books in this room?" Invite the kids to look around the room for places that might make sense, and perhaps you'll make a few suggestions to get the ideas flowing. "What about 'How to Wash Your Hands' next to the sink?" you might say, knowing full well that one of your students has written that very how-to book. "What about a basket of how-to books in our classroom library? How many of you might want to put one of your how-to books in there? Or what about hanging some on our class writing bulletin board?"

Enjoy!

Lucy, Beth, and Laurie

Session 7

Writers Reflect and Set Goals to Create Their Best Information Writing

THE SIMPLE ACT of noticing and naming the work that each child has done pays off in a number of important ways. Doing this makes the work more memorable and replicable and gives children vocabulary for talking and thinking about their own writing. That is why teaching children to look back over their own writing again and again is crucial. Periodically, in any unit, you will want to take time for kids to reread the work in their writing folders, pointing to, naming, and talking about the texts they have written so far—and to make plans for those they intend to write in the near future.

By now your children have written many how-to books, and they have had plenty of practice with several of the key features of the genre. With each new book, the process is becoming more automatic, and the quality of the writing is elevated.

As mentioned in earlier sessions, the Common Core State Standards offer a vision for what kindergarten informational writing can be. According to the standards, kindergartners will "use a combination of drawing, dictating, and writing to compose informative/explanatory texts in which they name what they are writing about and supply some information about the topic." This works with how-to book writing as well as it does with other types of informational writing. How will your children know if they are approaching this goal as they write how-to books?

In this lesson, you will help the children pause to reflect on the work they've done so far. To help children concretely understand the concept of reflection, we suggest showing them two examples of one student's work that clearly illustrate how that student's writing has grown over time. In this session we compare the how-to book of a child who is now in first grade to a how-to book he wrote in kindergarten. You could just as easily use one of your own student's pieces of writing from September to compare to the work the child is doing now or even create two contrasting examples of writing yourself. In any case, your goal in this lesson is to highlight that writers grow—a lot. And they grow because they set goals for themselves and they work hard to get there.

In this lesson, the children use star stickers to mark the spots in their writing where they are already meeting the expectations. The power is not in the stickers, of course, but

IN THIS SESSION, you'll teach students that writers draw on all they have learned about information writing, and they use an information writing checklist to set writing goals.

GETTING READY

✔ Student writing folders (see Connection)

✔ Information Writing Checklist, Grades K and 1 (see Connection) 💿

✔ Enlarged copies of two pieces of student work from a former student (if possible), one from kindergarten and one from first grade. Student work from a current student could be substituted here (see Teaching).

✔ A strip of eight gold star stickers for each student as well as some for you to demonstrate with. Colored pen, marker, other labels, or stickers could be substituted (See Active Engagement).

✔ Personal copies of the Information Writing Checklist for kids (see Active Engagement) 💿

COMMON CORE STATE STANDARDS: W.K.2, W.K.5, W.1.2, RI.K.1, RFS.K.1.b; RFS.K.3, RFS.1.3, SL.K.1, SL.K.2, SL.K.3, L.K.1, L.K.2.c,d; L.K.6

in the idea that we can concretely mark places in our writing that illustrate certain qualities. If you prefer, instead of stickers, you could give children special colored pens and invite them to underline or circle or star particular places in pieces of writing that show that they have tried each of the elements of strong informational writing.

"The simple act of noticing and naming the work that each child has done makes the work more memorable and replicable and gives children vocabulary for talking and thinking about their own writing."

This lesson is unusual in that you will be guiding children step by step to notice each of the items on the Information Writing Checklist from Unit 1. Usually in minilessons, you show a quick example and then send writers off to work on their own.

Of course, there will be items on the list that some children have not yet incorporated into their independent work. This is actually the most important part of the lesson: helping children to identify and record these goals. One way to help children keep track of their goals is to give each child a mini version of the Information Writing Checklist so that they might point to, or even mark, the items on the list they want to keep working on. Given kindergartners' love of stickers, you might say, for example, "If you can't find a place in your writing where you wrote words to tell about your pictures, you can put a star sticker on your mini chart to remind you to keep working on that! You can keep it in your writing folder to remind you of the things you want to keep working on every day as a writer."

You may decide to go one step further and use homemade labels with icons for each item on the list. You might use a heart for "I told what my topic was," or an easel or chalkboard for "I put different things I know about the topic on my page," or an exclamation point for "I told, drew, and wrote some important things about the topic." As you coach students to find the places in their writing where they have done these things, you can observe to see who in your class places a label even thought they haven't yet accomplished the goal. This is a teachable moment.

Being explicit is incredibly helpful and important. You will want to make it known that the items on the list are indeed the goals of the unit and that the ultimate goal would be to find *all* of the items in *every* piece of writing. The link in today's lesson is a message to the children as well as a reminder to you: "Now that you've reflected on all the work you've accomplished so far, decide on some of the things you need to keep working on. We still have plenty of time in this unit for everybody to get all of these into all their writing. Let's get started now!"

Writers Reflect and Set Goals to Create Their Best Information Writing

CONNECTION

Remind students that writers hold onto and use things they've already learned.

"Writers, bring your folders and come to the meeting area," I said, and once the children were gathered on the carpet, I began. "Do you remember last month, when we were writing true stories, I reminded you that even when you are learning many new things, you also need to remember that you *already know how* to do many things? Remember that? We looked at our old charts and used them to help us remember to do everything that we already knew *and* to do all the new things too. This is an important thing to do no matter what kind of writing you're doing. We can do it with our how-to books, too!

"When I was going through old charts, not only did I find the old 'How to Write a True Story' chart, but I also found the Information Writing Checklist. Do you remember when we made this way back at the beginning of the year?" (See p. 53; the full-size Information Writing Checklist can be found on the CD-ROM.)

Briefly review the old chart with your students to make sure it's fresh in their minds, keeping in mind that you will be going through the list again in detail shortly.

"Right now, let's read this chart together and try to remember when we first learned to do all of these important things."

I quickly read each item on the chart aloud, pausing for children to have a chance to think back, saying, "Thumbs up if you remember way back in September when we first learned this."

❖ **Name the teaching point.**

"Today I want to teach you that even though you are learning all these important new things about how-to books, you still need to remember everything you already learned about writing informational books. You can use old charts to help you keep track of all the work you are already doing and to help you set new goals."

◆ COACHING

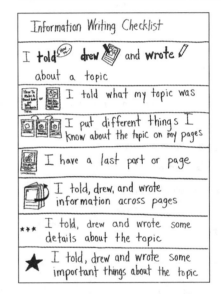

FIG. 7–1 Your kindergarteners will benefit from picture support added to the Information Writing Checklist. This chart can remain on display throughout the remainder of the unit as a tool for checking in on goals for information writing. The chart used in this session does not include the Conventions section of the complete checklist, because conventions will be highlighted later in the unit.

This is essentially the same teaching point you taught early in the Writing for Readers *unit. Strong teaching often revisits strategies again and again in new contexts.*

TEACHING

Using two pieces of student writing that illustrate growth over time, highlight the idea that writers grow when they set goals and work toward them.

"This morning when I was walking down the hall to our classroom, one of my old students who is in first grade now, Luke, came running up to me. Some of you know him, don't you? Well, Luke was all excited because his class had just finished writing all-about books, and he couldn't wait to show me. He took me over to his class's bulletin board in the hallway, and I read his writing, and you know what? It was a-ma-zing how much Luke had grown as a writer, and he told me it was because he was always setting goals for himself and had worked really, really hard to reach them. I was so proud of him. In fact, when I got to our room this morning I looked through my old files and I found an old, old piece of Luke's writing from last year, and I asked him if I could share it with you guys, so you could see how much you can grow from kindergarten to first grade."

I had taped a photocopy of Luke's kindergarten writing on chart paper, above a photocopy of his latest first-grade writing. The difference was obvious.

Step 1: First take the connector and plug it in next . . . Be careful. Do not push too hard.

Step 2: Open the DVD holder next . . . Do not put your finger in the DVD holder.

Step 3: Put the DVD in next . . .

Step 4: Turn on the TV next . . .

Step 5: You play Play Station 2.

  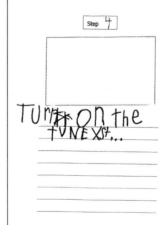  

FIG. 7–2   Luke's piece from kindergarten

Positions

In football there is a lot of positions in football. One position is a quarterback. A quarterback's job is to throw the ball and run the ball and snap the ball. The kicker kicks the ball for a field goal or return the ball.

Gear

In football you need gear. A type of gear is football pants. Another type of gear is a helmet. Another is shoulder pads. Another is a cup. Another is cleats. Oh, and wait. I meant a football cup, not a real cup.

Equipment

In football you need equipment. One type of equipment is a football. Another is a field goal. Another is a field.

Team

In football there are teams. One team is the Texas Longhorns. Another is the New England Patriots. Another is the Jets. Another is the Giants. Another is the Baltimore Ravens. Another is the Dallas Cowboys.

Closing

Now you know all about football. See you on the field. Do not forget your cup.

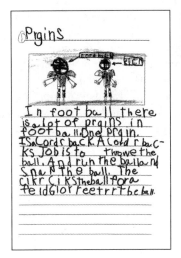

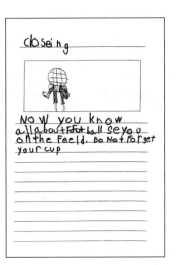

FIG. 7–3   Luke's piece from first grade

After the giggling had subsided (yes, Luke's piece was funny), I continued. "Wow. What do you notice? Turn and tell your partner." I listened in as partners began to talk.

"I know! It's really incredible isn't it? How many of you noticed that Luke used to write just a little bit on each page, but now you can see that he really says a lot of information for every page?" Nearly all of the kids' hands flew up. "You know what? I'm going to put a little note here for Luke, a little star sticker to let him know that we noticed that he's really writing a lot of information on each page. Don't you think he would like that?"

I peeled off a star sticker and stuck it right on a particularly detailed portion of the drawing.

Suggest that students use the Information Writing Checklist to determine which writing goals they have met and which they can work toward, making note of each in a concrete way.

"I noticed that some of you weren't sure what to look for in Luke's writing. Hey, couldn't we use our Information Writing Checklist to look at Luke's writing? Let's try that together. I'll go down the checklist, and you go like this with your hands to show me if we could give Luke a star for it." I made a star gesture by bunching my hand in a fist, and then spreading it out again, like a shooting star. "Why don't you all give it a try now?"

Referring to the checklist and Luke's older piece of writing, I asked, "How many of you noticed that Luke put different things he knows about a topic across the pages? Don't say anything. Just remember our star sign!" The kids unanimously gave him the star gesture, something that I now (happily) realized was going to live in our classroom for quite a while. I peeled off another star and stuck it on his writing. The kids were rapt. It was obvious to me now that the whole class was wondering, "Are we going to get to use stickers?"

I pointed out that Luke had also made a final page for his how-to, to let us know when all the steps were done, the fourth item on our checklist. Another star. I moved on to the next item on the list, "I told, drew, and wrote information across the pages." I stopped. "Huh. I'm not so sure about this one. He has a lot of information in his words, but there are no pictures! There is a lot more he could have shown. What should I do?" The kids looked a little concerned. I could tell what they were thinking, "No star? But we like giving stars!"

"Hey, I know what we could do!" I pulled out a smaller version of the Information Writing Checklist that I had already prepared. "We could give him a copy of our chart, like this, to let him know some things he could keep working on—so he can reach for more stars!" I read the line on the card, "I told, drew, and wrote about a topic," and stuck a star next to it. "What do you guys think about that?" "Yes!" the kids shouted.

ACTIVE ENGAGEMENT

Tell students they will be noting goals accomplished and goals to work toward.

"So, writers, how would you like to give yourselves some stars to show what goals you've accomplished and which ones you're working toward? Right now, I'm going to give each of you some special star stickers and your own copy

When you introduce the Information Writing Checklist to your class, you might want to begin with the items that are most familiar, or that lend themselves to the particular piece of writing you are using. I decided not to begin at the top of the list, because I knew that it would be easier for children to recognize that yes, Luke did put different things that he knows.

Telling, drawing, and writing are all included in the Information Writing Checklist because all three are important expectations for kindergarteners to demonstrate in their work. You might discover that children in your class are leaning heavily on one or the other, instead of utilizing all three. When a child or group of children (or whole class) needs extra support in any one of the three, then that becomes a goal to teach into in a conference, small group, or minilesson.

of the Information Writing Checklist that you can use to keep track of the goals you're still working toward. We're going to go down the checklist together to see which items on the list are goals you've met (you'll put stars right in your books where you notice those goals) and which items on the list are goals you're still working toward. You'll stick those stars on your own copy of the Information Writing Checklist."

I passed a strip of eight stars to each student (one star for each item on the checklist, plus one extra), plus small copies of the Kindergarten and First Grade Information Writing Checklists that I had already prepared.

Guide the children through the checklist step by step, showing them how to mark their how-to books where they have accomplished a goal and how to mark their card when they are still working toward a goal.

"Let's begin with 'I told, drew, and wrote about a topic.' Right now, look through your folder and choose a piece that shows you did this." I paused while children selected a piece of writing. "Let's make sure. Thumbs up if you can *tell* out loud the information in your how-to. Great. Thumbs up if you *drew* pictures that teach the steps on all your pages. Nice. Okay, now thumbs up if you also *wrote* the steps on each page. Excellent. If you gave yourself a thumbs-up for all of these, stick a star on that piece of writing! If you didn't draw all your pictures or if you didn't write words yet—just stick the star right onto your mini-copy of our Information Writing Checklist to remind yourself to work on it." I pointed to the bigger copy of the checklist to show them where that star would go.

I continued on to the next item on the checklist in the same fashion, and the next, sometimes moving around to coach children who seemed puzzled, occasionally suggesting to particular children that they mark their checklist instead of just putting the star anywhere. I knew that over time, the checklist would become very familiar to kids, as I planned on using it often in conferences and small groups to help kids figure out what to work on.

"Writers, I am so proud of all of you. Look at how much you already know how to do as writers. There is just one last thing. Remember I said I was going to teach you to use the chart to keep track of all that you are doing *and* to help you set goals? Lots of you already marked your checklist with one or two things to work on. Now everyone should have one last sticker left. Right now, if you haven't marked anything on your checklist yet, either pick one thing to reach for, or you could even write something on your list. You could put a question mark there if you aren't sure what to work on, or you could pick something from our other charts to work on."

Information Writing Checklist

	Kindergarten	NOT YET	STARTING TO	YES!	Grade 1	NOT YET	STARTING TO	YES!
	Structure				**Structure**			
Overall	I told, drew, and wrote about a topic.	☐	☐	☐	I taught my readers about a topic.	☐	☐	☐
Lead	I told what my topic was.	☐	☐	☐	I named my topic in the beginning and got my readers' attention.	☐	☐	☐
Transitions	I put different things I knew about the topic on my pages.	☐	☐	☐	I told different parts about my topic on different pages.	☐	☐	☐
Ending	I had a last part or page.	☐	☐	☐	I wrote an ending.	☐	☐	☐
Organization	I told, drew, and wrote information across pages.	☐	☐	☐	I told about my topic part by part.	☐	☐	☐
	Development				**Development**			
Elaboration	I drew and wrote important things about the topic.	☐	☐	☐	I put facts in my writing to teach about my topic.	☐	☐	☐
Craft	I told, drew, and wrote some details about the topic.	☐	☐	☐	I used labels and words to give facts.	☐	☐	☐
	Language Conventions				**Language Conventions**			
Spelling	I could read my writing.	☐	☐	☐	I used all I knew about words and chunks (*at, op, it,* etc.) to help me spell.	☐	☐	☐
	I wrote a letter for the sounds I heard.	☐	☐	☐	I spelled the word wall words right and used the word wall to help me spell other words.	☐	☐	☐
	I used the word wall to help me spell.	☐	☐	☐				

As children move through the grades, the work they do each year will stand on the shoulders of years' past. For today's session, you might adapt the kindergarten and first-grade checklist to contain as many or as few items as needed. You might also use the first-grade checklist as an alternative if it is a better fit for the characteristics of your young writers. Try to avoid using a checklist where children will simply check off everything as "done." On the other hand, you won't want a checklist where the children have nothing at all to check off.

LINK

Before sending them off to work, ask students to use the Information Writing Checklist to tell their writing partners what they plan to work on.

"Writers, this year all of you are going to grow as writers just as much as Luke did. And it all starts right now. Last year, Luke was just like you, and he kept setting goals and working on them, just like you did today. You've just given yourself stars for all the great things you already know how to do, and you also have a few things to reach for. Right now, turn to the person next to you and use the stars that you placed on your checklist to tell them what you are going to work on today, and every day, in your writing."

If you find that reflecting on every item on the checklist is going to take too long, you might do part of the checklist in the minilesson, and the rest of the checklist during a mid-workshop teaching point, or the share.

Information Writing Checklist Scully

I **told** **drew** and **wrote** about a topic

I told what my topic was

I put different things I know about the topic on my pages

I have a last part or page

I told, drew, and wrote information across pages

★★★ I told, drew and wrote some details about the topic

★ I told, drew and wrote some important things about the topic

Scully has marked his checklist with a star to show that he plans to work on telling, drawing, and writing details about his topic.

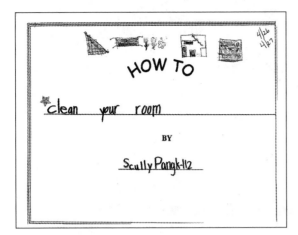

HOW TO

clean your room

BY

Scully Pangk-112

4/26
4/27

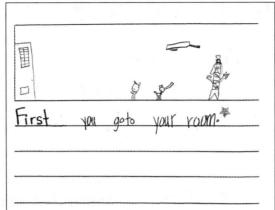

First you go to your room.

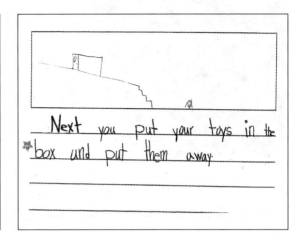

Next you put your toys in the box and put them away.

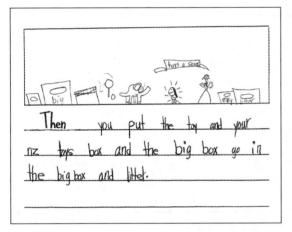

Then you put the toy and your nz toys box and the big box go in the big box and littel.

Then you clan you all the room in the room and you clean up evd in your room.

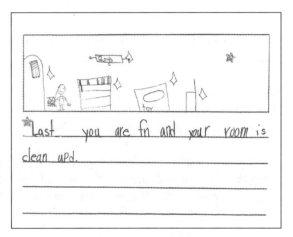

Last you are fn and your room is clean upd.

FIG 7–4   With the help of a teacher, Scully decides that his writing could use more detail. Future lessons on elaboration and using detail in the pictures to fuel more writing will help Scully become a more detailed writer.

Helping Writers Keep Everything They've Learned in Mind as They Work

I HAD CONFERRED WITH JONATHAN at the beginning of work time about adding more details to his drawings so that readers would really be able to picture the steps of his how-to book about making a Lego space ship. His drawings had been so spare it was hard to see a difference between steps. Knowing that Jonathan's drawing skill had increased dramatically since the beginning of the year when he was not yet drawing representationally, I pushed for more detail and clarity in his how-to book drawings. He was game and immediately started adding details.

After conferring with a couple more students, I circled back around to check on Jonathan and discovered that he was still on the same page of his how-to book! That page was packed with details. But that was all he had done since I'd seen him last.

Whenever we introduce something new, sometimes children focus on that one thing to the exclusion of everything else they've learned. This is completely normal. The pendulum swings hard in the direction of the new learning. It can take some time—and some reminders from you—to bring back the balance.

I knelt down by Jonathan and said, "Wow, Jonathan, you sure have been working hard on adding details to your pictures. Your readers have so much more information now! It will be a lot easier for them to understand how to make this ship. Jonathan beamed.

"Can I see what you've worked on on the other pages of your book?" I asked this knowing that Jonathan had not, in fact, even turned the page, but the question implied that there was other work to be done.

"I just was adding details to here," he said. "See the number? It's spaceship 5!"

"This is so great, Jonathan," I said. "You really are helping your readers by adding more details to that picture. But here's the thing. I know I reminded you that writers add important details to their pictures today, but that doesn't mean that adding details is the *only* work you do today. Right? Writers have so many things to keep in mind, and

MID-WORKSHOP TEACHING
Writers Want Feedback on Their Hard Work

"Writers, eyes up here for a moment, please. When writers work very hard and have tried to make their writing the best they've ever written, they want to get feedback on their work. They want to hear what they've done well, but they also want to hear things that can make their books even better. Using your best teaching voice, will Partner 1 read the how-to book that you think is your best to Partner 2? Then, partners, please give feedback. Don't just say, 'I like your book.' Say, 'I like your how-to book because I was able to follow your directions,' or 'I like your how-to book because I could read it clearly.'"

sometimes when you are working on one thing, you can forget about all of the other things we've been learning about and practicing."

This elicited a large sigh from Jonathan. "Don't be discouraged! You're doing such grown-up work. You really focused on trying out adding more details. That's huge! But I want to remind you that writers also keep in mind all the other things they know. What else have we been working on that you could think about as you finish your book?"

"It's gotta make sense," he offered.

"So true!" I said. "Maybe you could read through it and see if the steps make sense and if your words have as many details as your pictures. But that's just one idea. I want to remind you that when writers are working, they keep in mind not just *one* thing they've learned, but *all* of the things they've been learning."

Jonathan flipped back to the beginning of his book and started rereading.

Getting How-To Books into Readers' Hands

To create a mini-celebration, suggest that writers distribute their how-to books to appropriate places around the room and the school.

"Writers, I know we usually don't put our writing out on shelves for people to read until the end of the unit, but some of your how-to books could be useful to this class right now. Remember yesterday when I mentioned that we'd be putting some of your how-to books out so that people could actually start using them? Like this book about how to clean a hamster cage. I don't think we should wait to put it into a place where people will find it when they need it. A book on how to jump on a trampoline could go in the how-to book basket we made for our classroom library or maybe on the how-to book bulletin board in the hall. I'm thinking that first you'll need to choose two of your how-to books, books that you think people will be able to start using right away, and then work together to figure out where you can put them in the school so that they'll be really useful. Are you game?"

Of course they were! As children spoke with their writing partners about where they wanted to put their how-to books, I started taping some of the how-to books to their chosen spots. As children saw me do this, they were inspired to think of new places to put how-to books, and soon there were books everywhere. "How to Wash Your Hands" was hanging right by the sink in the classroom. "How to Do a Fire Drill" went by the door (see Figure 7–5 on next page). "How to Shop for Books" was placed right by the classroom library, and "How to Be Principal for the Day" was on its way to being hung on the door in the principal's office.

How to __do a findril__

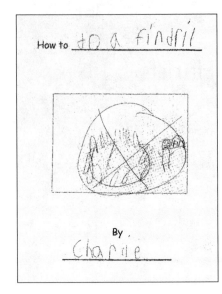

By . Charlie

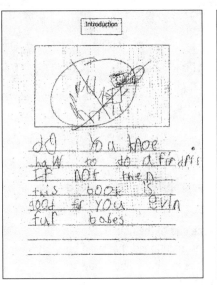

do You knoe haw to do a firdril If not then this book is good for you evin fur babes

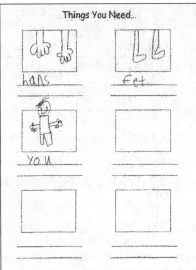

hans   fet

you

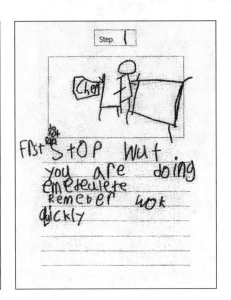

FIrst stOp wut you are doing emedeulete remeber wok qickly

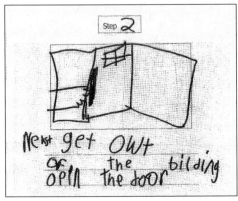

Nekst get owt of the bilding opln the door

Nekst wat 5 minlts and then go bak in

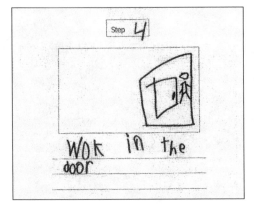

Wok in the door

Tien You ken go bat to wat you wrdoing

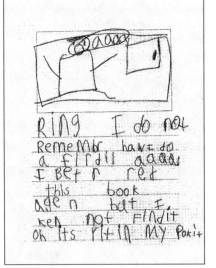

RIng I do not RememBr hawt do a firdil aaaa I Bet r ret this book aden but I ken not FINdit oh Its ritiln My Pokit

FIG. 7–5   Charlie's Fire Drill How-To book

Writers Emulate Features of Informational Writing Using a Mentor Text

IN THIS SESSION, you'll teach students that writers study mentor texts: noticing, naming, and trying out what they discover.

GETTING READY

✔ Ahead of time, read aloud and discuss *My First Soccer Game* by Alyssa Satin Capucilli so that it will already be familiar (see Connection)

✔ Chart paper and markers to create new chart: "Learning from a Mentor How-To Text" (see Active Engagement)

✔ Class shared writing from Bend I, about making a peanut butter and jelly sandwich (see Active Engagement)

✔ Basket of how-to books, containing books by published professional authors as well as ones by student authors, set out on tables (see Link)

✔ "How-To Writing" anchor chart on display

F OR TWO WEEKS NOW, your children have been writing books that teach readers how to do something. The children have had a mini-celebration of these how-to books, "publishing" some of their work by putting it around the room for others to read. They are proud to be authors of this new kind of writing, showing off their teaching and writing expertise.

In this next bend in the unit, you teach children to reach new heights by working under the influence of a published, masterful how-to text. That is, you'll help children study a mentor text, something they have done before and will do in almost every unit, and you'll help them apply what they learn to their own writing.

Emulating another writer's work is not easy: how do you copy but not copy? It is helpful, however, to show youngsters a book or two that has easy-to-emulate features that they are bound to notice and bound to want to try in their own writing.

We recommend *My First Soccer Game*, by Alyssa Satin Capucilli. Most children will notice this how-to book aims to help readers learn to play soccer. The book contains a list of what is needed to play. This feature of a how-to text is much like the lists of ingredients accompanying recipes in a cookbook. Readers will also notice that the pictures in this book are explicit teaching pictures. These diagram-illustrations can be contrasted with typical illustrations. Youngsters will notice that the steps are distinctly numbered. Of course, there will be some features that are not necessarily critical for children to notice and emulate. For example, some words in this text are written in bold font, and there's hardly a child on this earth who doesn't take that up before anything else! In this text, the bold words are not the sound effects, but instead tend to be the domain-specific vocabulary.

COMMON CORE STATE STANDARDS: W.K.2, W.K.5, W.1.2, RI.K.1, RI.K.7, RI.1.1, RI.1.7, SL.K.1, SL.K.2, SL.K.3, L.K.1, L.K.2

Writers Emulate Features of Informational Writing Using a Mentor Text

CONNECTION

Tell children that their how-to books inspired you to read more of that genre and that you found yourself reading differently because you've been a *writer* of how-to books.

"The other day, when I read all your how-to books, I learned so many things that I didn't know how to do before. I learned how to make a friendship pin, how to ride a scooter, how to blow bubbles, and even how to make a smoothie. Your writing made me want to read even more how-to books! So, I went to the library and found some new how-to books.

"I made myself a little pile, and I started reading one in a regular way, like I read every other kind of book, but after I read just the first page, I found myself saying, 'Holy moly! *Look* what this writer did! That is so cool. I'm going to definitely try the exact same thing in my book.'

"You already know that writers find books that are a lot like the ones they want to write and study them. But the really important thing is that writers read those books in a special way. Instead of just reading along through the pages, page after page after page, writers read just a little and then stop and think, 'Oh my goodness. *Look* what this author did!' And writers say to themselves, 'I could try the exact same thing!' And then, they do just that!

"Today, instead of a regular minilesson, we're going to explore something together. We will be researching a question as a class."

I held up a book that we'd read several times already, *My First Soccer Game*. "Here is a book we know really well and love a lot."

Name the inquiry question.

"So here is the question: What are some things that Alyssa Satin Capucilli does as a writer that I might try, and why does she do those things?"

There is a saying, "Give someone a fish, they eat for a day. Teach someone to fish, they eat for a lifetime." The purpose of this guided inquiry into My First Soccer Game *isn't just to teach kids the features of how-to books. It's to teach them how to dig into a text they want to emulate, notice features and craft moves, and then learn how to incorporate their noticings into their own writing. First and foremost, our goal is to teach a process.*

It is crucial that children are already familiar with the chosen book before you use it as a mentor text in writing lessons. Otherwise, your class will likely focus all their attention on understanding the content of the book (in this case soccer), instead of thinking about the craft and style of writing. We suggest reading aloud and discussing the content of the book ahead of time, not during a minilesson.

INQUIRY SET-UP

Set children up for a mini-inquiry; set them up to study this mentor text for something they could try in their own writing.

"We can study this book together and figure out what the author has done that we could try. This is something writers do all the time: they let themselves be taught by other writers! Remember when we learned from Phyllis Root's book, *Creak! Said the Bed*? Here, let's take a look at this page from Alyssa's book and read it together. As we read, let's stop and notice some of the things that Alyssa does as a writer. Also, we'll see if we can imagine why she does those things."

ACTIVE ENGAGEMENT

Read aloud a selection of the mentor text, encouraging children to notice text features. Make sure all students can see the text well (project it or pass out copies).

"I'm going to read these two pages, and then will you turn to your partner and talk about what this how-to author did that you could do too?" I read the title page aloud and then began reading the text.

I stopped after the first page. "So I'm noticing this is about soccer and all the stuff—No, *wait*. Talking about *the topic* of soccer isn't going to help us, is it? We need to notice *what she does to write this* that other people could do too—not what her writing is about, but *how* she writes it. Hmm. Let's read it again and think about *how* she writes.

"Ball, cleats, soccer. All of these are things that you need to play soccer." I paused here. "Are you thinking with me about *how* she writes?" I reread once again, this time noting the items she listed across my fingers, hoping the children would notice the text begins with a list of what people need.

I read on. "'One.'" I emphasized the number, pausing, to help children hear the number itself—to help them notice numbered steps as a text feature. Then I continued reading.

"'This is going to be a great day . . . Step 1. Follow the **leader**! **Jog** or **run slowly** in a circle with your friends.'

"Now that we've read the first few pages, turn to your partner and talk about what you noticed that Alyssa did that you could try in your own writing." I gave them a moment to talk and plan. As they spoke, I coached. "What else do you notice? Why do you think she did that?"

As children discussed *My First Soccer Game* I got up from my spot (as I often do during the active engagement) and circulated among the kids to listen in and coach.

I heard Destiny say to Roberto, "I notice there are numbers for the steps."

"Yeah, just like us," replied Roberto.

I leaned in to the two partners and held the book up a little closer, "What else do you notice about her pictures and her words that you might be able to try?"

"Well…" said Roberto, searching the page. Then his eyes hit upon something. "Oh! I know! Look! Those words are darker!"

Although my first impulse was to join in Roberto's excitement, I knew that if I spoke now, the conversation would become an exchange between Roberto and me, instead of the two partners, Destiny and Roberto. I waited to see what Destiny's reply would be, and looked at her questioningly, pointing to a spot on the page where bold words appeared.

"Oh… I see it now too." After a brief pause, she smiled and pointed in the book. "And it's here, and here too."

With our time for discussion at its end, I reconvened the class so that we could create a chart compiling some of what they had noticed. I knew that many kids would begin to understand how to study a mentor text once they heard several examples.

Ask children to report on their findings and chart them with quick picture clues for easy reference later.

"Think about all you have said and choose something you might add to a new chart we're making today to go along with our 'How-To Writing' chart. This new one will help us keep track of all we are *learning from a mentor how-to text*. Thumbs up if you have something to add."

When many children had their thumbs up, I said, "While you were talking with your partners I overheard some amazing ideas we could add. Let me tell you what I heard, and put a thumb up if you and your partner noticed that very same thing." I listed the following elements of Alyssa's how-to book, making sure to emphasize *why* the author might have made those choices.

Often, the charts you create will include some of what children actually said and some of your own contributions to make the chart as useful and instructive as possible.

> Learning from a Mentor How-To Text
>
> 1. The title tells the reader what the book is about
>
> 2. Pictures that teach
>
> 3. List of things you need
>
> 4. Important parts in **bold**

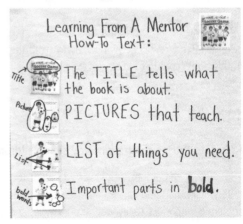

FIG. 8–1 Photocopies of select portions of the mentor text make this chart easy for your young writers to understand.

"Wow! That's a lot of new ideas to add to our new chart! Should I write them in?" The kids agreed, so I quickly added them.

   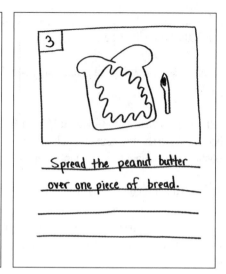

FIG. 8–2 The class-shared text can grow bit by bit as new strategies are learned.

Ask children to apply something from the chart to a class piece of how-to writing.

"These are such great ideas! Let's think about which ones might make our book about how to make a peanut butter and jelly sandwich stronger." I held up the now-familiar book.

"Would number 1, the how-to book title, help me make our book stronger? What do you think? Want to give it a try?" Without further ado, the class named the book "How to Make a Peanut Butter and Jelly Sandwich."

"Wow—seems like adding a title will help make our book, 'How to Make a Peanut Butter and Jelly Sandwich,' even stronger. Readers will know right away what they are going to learn to do. We could try out lots of things on the chart in this book, couldn't we?"

LINK

Reiterate the teaching point and send children off to study mentor texts.

"So, writers, remember, whenever you want to learn to do something better, you can learn from someone who does it very well. Then you can try what he or she has done! If you want to learn to kick a ball even farther, you can watch someone who kicks really well and try what she does. If you want to learn how to whistle all kinds of notes, you can watch someone who whistles really well and try what he does. And the same is true if you want to make your how-to books even better. You can study authors who write very well and try what they do.

As with any mentor text, you will want to make sure to highlight what the author does—and why she does it, so that children will begin to understand that the author has a purpose behind every craft move.

How to Trick People with
Bertie Bott's Beans by Kurt

Read this book to trick
people.

Step 1: Get a Jellybean box.

Step 2: Ask somebody, Do you
want to have this bean?

Say, I **dare** you to eat this
bean. That is how to <u>trick</u>
people.

FIG. 8–3 This student applies what he's learned from the mentor text to his own how-to books.

"Today use all that you've been doing and also try something from our new chart, 'Learning from a Mentor How-To Text.' You could either go back and revise a how-to book you've already written or use the chart to help you write a new one. There are how-to books on your tables. Spend a few minutes studying them and noticing what cool things those authors are doing. Maybe you'll find something that you want to try out!"

You may be concerned at the idea of a class full of youngsters, each independently studying the features of nonfiction writing. Relax! Let the children approximate this as well as they can. It doesn't really matter that children notice any particular characteristics. It does matter that they have time to explore, to talk, to notice, and to rev themselves up for this new endeavor.

Using Mentor Texts to Confer

BECAUSE YOU HAVE JUST BEGUN A BEND IN THE ROAD that is dedicated to the idea of learning from mentor texts, you may want to think of today as a day in which you confer with a book under your arm. To prepare for that conferring, you can inch through your mentor text, using Post-its to mark some of the choices you notice the author has made that could be informative to children. For example, you can start with the cover and note that the cover includes not just a title but the author's name. Inside the front cover, there is a dedication and a list of other books by this author. What a treasure trove of information, right there!

Of course, you may question whether those features are really all that essential. Is it crucial for, say, Melissa to include a page titled, "Other books by Melissa"? Of course not. But on the other hand, it is absolutely critical that you help children see themselves as writers. They'll read everything they encounter—and experience everything—differently if they do so from the perspective of "I am one who writes." And yes, noticing that a published book contains a listing of other titles by an author and deciding to include that feature in one's own writing can absolutely help a child to self-identify as a writer.

As you continue inching through your mentor how-to book, you'll probably make note of a diagram or two, hopefully one with clear and specific labels. If you're using *My First Soccer Game*, you'll spot the diagram of a soccer field and its features. For example, players are labeled using the terms of the game—in this instance, the titles of their roles: right defender, left forward, and so forth.

When you imagine the teaching possibilities *My First Soccer Game* offers, you'll note that the book has flaps. That will, of course, appeal to children. These are not considered a standard feature of how-to texts, but you can use them as an example as you explain to children that authors are always coming up with their very own ideas for how to make readers want to read a book. Alyssa decided that flaps were right for her book, and you can encourage young writers to come up with their own innovations to attract readers.

The mentor texts you carry with you as you confer will not, of course, determine the course of your conferences. You'll confer as usual, researching what the writer is doing and then thinking, "What can I teach that might help?" Having studied the text in advance, it's likely that you'll find something in the text that will perfectly illustrate the teaching point you want to make.

MID-WORKSHOP TEACHING   **Collecting Ideas from Mentor Texts: Using Capital Letters for Emphasis**

"Writers, eyes on me. As they were looking at the how-to books in their basket, Rebecca and Sam noticed that the how-to book they were reading has words written in all capital letters for the parts that are loud or exciting. That works kind of like bolds, right? I'll add this to our list as you all get back to work. I bet you're all noticing other things we can add to the chart later as well. At this point, if you haven't already shifted from studying other authors' books to working on your own, it's time. You can go back to old books and add in new features to make them better, or you can start a new book and include something new."

As the children got back to work, I added "ALL CAPS" to the chart.

As Students Continue Working . . .

"Jennifer just discovered something cool that the author of the book she's reading is doing—adding flaps! But listen, everyone, you don't have to ask me before trying out something you discover in a book. Just go for it! Make sure to tell me what you tried, later, but you don't need to wait for me to get started!"

Writers Can All Be Mentor Authors

Suggest that children can study features in each others' books as well as in the books of published mentor authors. Organize one child to read his or her books aloud to a small group while listeners note features.

"Writers, your books have so many wonderful features that help your readers to actually do the thing you are teaching. I am realizing that people do not need to study just Alyssa's mentor text to learn about features. People can study *your* books to learn about features. Let's have you and your partner work with another set of partners or two. 'Scoodle' over to another partnership. I'll wait a minute while you get settled.

"In a minute, I'm going to ask one writer from each group to read aloud his or her how-to book while the rest of you listen. I'll come around quickly and tap the reader on the shoulder. But first, listeners, pay attention to the kind of features the writer uses. When the writer is done reading, tell what features you noticed. Maybe you will get ideas for what you can do in your writing by noticing what your classmate has done.

"Okay, I'm going to tap one person from each group to read your book aloud." As I quickly zipped around, I made sure to tap children who had included a variety of features in their how-to books. As I sat back down, I continued, "Today, as your friends read their how-to books, your job will be to pay attention to what these writers did that you might want to try out."

As the readers began, I moved around listening in. After Jonathan finished, his reviewers said, "You used steps, you used teaching pictures, you used diagrams. But you didn't give your book a title."

"Oh, I was going to do that. It's 'How to Get Ready for School!'" Jonathan responded, as though he had thought of it on his own.

Remind writers that they can always think about which features they have used and which they might want to try as they write how-to books.

Calling the students back together, I said, "Writers, I want to remind you that you can pay attention to features as you read over your own how-to books. Look at our chart and ask yourself, 'What features did I use? What other features am I planning to use?' Remember, the choice is yours, but you always want to make sure that you are including a lot of features to teach your topic."

Writing for Readers

Using the Word You

IN THIS SESSION, you'll teach students that writers focus in on their audience by addressing readers directly, using *you*.

GETTING READY

✔ Children's writing folders and pencils (see Connection)

✔ "How-To Writing" anchor chart as well as copies for each student (see Connection)

✔ "Learning from a Mentor How-To Text" chart (see Connection and Link)

✔ *My First Soccer Game* by Alyssa Satin Capucilli (see Teaching and Share)

✔ Post-its (see Share)

COMMON CORE STATE STANDARDS: W.K.2, RI.K.1, SL.K.1, SL.K.5, L.K.1, L.K.2, L.K.6, L.1.1.j,d

WRITERS OF PROCEDURAL TEXTS (how-to texts) have a special obligation to readers. These are the writers whose readers are on hands and knees, reaching behind the VCR, or standing by the stove with frying pan in hand. Because how-to writing is all about providing readers with the direction they need, when they need it, it should not surprise you that this session again helps youngsters to work toward writing in ways that reach readers. This time, the spin that you put on this is to help writers to write in direct address. That is, you are helping writers to write to *you*, the reader. Doing so will keep writers from slipping back into the narrative voice and will help writers keep the reader—or the readers—in mind. Of course, the *you* may be one person or it may be a whole city full of people.

"The use of direct address not only helps a writer to keep the reader in mind but to assume an in-charge position."

This means helping writers write using the pronoun *you*, and of course, more than that, it means helping them to think of their writing as words that reach out to the reader, that take the hand of the reader and bring that reader along.

The use of direct address not only helps a writer to keep the reader in mind. It also helps the writer to assume an in-charge position. The writer is telling the reader what to do. "First you . . . Then you . . . After that you . . ." Or "You should . . ." Or "You must . . ." The simple strategy of referencing *you* and of speaking directly to the reader somehow packs a lot of punch.

Writing for Readers
Using the Word You

CONNECTION

Suggest that your class has learned enough to be ready to graduate from the old "How-To Writing" chart to the new "Learning from a Mentor How-To Text" chart.

"Writers, bring your folders today when you come to our meeting area." I said, and called each table to their spots at the carpet. When they had gathered, I began. "Writers, you've been writing how-to books every day, and you've written so many that I think you are ready to graduate. Have any of you ever been to a graduation? This is a celebration that happens when people finish one school and get ready for a higher-level school, a harder school. People wear flat hats with tassels on them and parade in to the song, 'Pomp and Circumstance.'" I hummed and pretended to be a graduate.

"You have all gotten so skilled at doing the things on our old 'How-To Writing' chart that I think you are ready to graduate to a whole new level. What that means is that you will leave the old chart behind and you'll graduate to now study a higher level, and harder level, of how-to books. Are you okay with that?"

Present small copies of the old chart to all the writers, calling these certificates attesting to all that children now know and do always.

"When people graduate, they are always given a fancy certificate, a fancy paper, that says, 'This is what you already know.' I'm going to give you each a fancy certificate that says, 'This is what you already know,' and you know what it will be? It will be your very own smaller copy of our old 'How-To Writing' chart!

"Keep this little copy in your folder to remind you of all the things you already studied and already know, because those will be things you do always. And we're going to move the big 'How-To Writing' chart over here so that you can still see it and replace it with our new mentor text chart that shows all the newest stuff we've been thinking about. What do you think? Does that make sense?"

Replace the old chart with a new anchor chart, putting it in a place of honor.

"Now, let's use our *new* chart to help us check in on our writing."

A little drama can add a lot to students' understanding and engagement. Don't be afraid to ham it up!

How-To Writing

1. Tells what to do, in **detailed** steps.

2. Numbers the steps.

3. Has a picture for each step.

4. Has labels that teach.

Scaffold students to use the chart as a guide, helping them to assess their writing to see if they've done each item that they admired in the mentor author's text.

"Let's try this together. Take out one of the how-to books you are working on now." Pointing to the first step on the chart, I said, "A title can let the reader know what your book will be about, but it can also remind you, the writer, to make sure that all your pages are connected. Check right now to see that all of the pages in your how-to book are connected to the title. If not, mark the pages that do not fit with an *R* for revise, so that you can remember to revise them today during writing workshop." I observed and circulated around the meeting area as children reread their how-to books, glancing over the titles children had given their books and doing spot checks to see that the steps of their how-to books were staying on topic.

"Writers, will each of you pick one more thing to work on—something you think might make your writing even better?" I quickly reread the chart. "Thumbs up when you've decided on one more thing to really think about as you work on your how-to books today."

I helped the writers check on one more item and then said, "Later today, you'll use this chart to help you check on all of these things, and whenever you see ways that you need to revise your writing, leave yourself a big note saying *R* for revise. Then you can go back and do that revision.

"Now, there is just one other thing I think you can do to make your writing *even* clearer. Sometimes writers write right *to their readers*. Let me tell you what I mean."

❖ **Name the teaching point.**

"Today I want to teach you that when you're writing a how-to book, your words need to reach your reader. And that reader might be standing there, with something half-made, half-done, waiting to hear what to do next. One of the best ways to reach your readers is to talk directly to them, by saying the word *you*: 'First you . . . and then you . . .'"

TEACHING

Recruit students to study the way a mentor author writes directly to the reader. Point out what the writer could have done but didn't to highlight the use of direct address.

"Writers, let's study how our mentor author uses her words to reach her readers. In a how-to book, the writer is writing to a reader who is trying to do something—to scramble an egg or to make a soccer goal. That reader might be standing by the hot frying pan with something half-made or getting ready to race out onto the soccer field, so you want your words to reach the reader, straight and true like an arrow.

"One of the best ways to reach your reader is to talk directly to the reader. Lots of writers of how-to books talk right to the reader, saying, 'First *you* . . . and then *you*. . . .'

If you want to give more sustained close-in support, you might not give writers the choice of the next item, and instead you might proceed through the chart. Pointing to step 2 on the chart, you could say, "We can also check to see that we've included pictures that teach. Flip back through your books and point to a place where you've done that—remembering that if you've forgotten this step, you can add it in later." You can continue to work your way through the anchor chart, item by item.

Learning from a Mentor How-To Text

1. The title tells the reader what the book is about

2. Pictures that teach

3. List of things you need

4. Important parts in **bold** or ALL CAPS

Speaking directly to the audience using you *communicates clearly. You may have noticed that this is the language in which most minilessons are delivered. Clear language makes clear teaching.*

"For example, Alyssa, *could* have just said, 'Some people run around. Some people lift their knees. Some people move their knees. Some people can stretch. Now some people can go play.'" I pointed to each section of the page as I read, using my voice to show that this was not the best way to give very clear directions.

"But Alyssa didn't write her directions that way, did she? No, she wrote right to me and to each of her readers. She said, 'Can *you* move *your* knees up and down like a butterfly flutters its wings?'" I emphasized *you* and *your* as I said this.

ACTIVE ENGAGEMENT

Recruit children to rehearse for their next book by trying to write-in-the-air directly to their partner, who assumes the role of reader, speaking to the partner as *you*.

"Now it's your turn to give this a try. Right now, think of the next how-to book you plan to write. When you've got an idea for a topic, give me a thumbs up." I paused and waited.

When most of the children were ready, I continued. "Now, Partner 2, please write your book in the air. This time, be sure you say the step to your partner very clearly so that your partner doesn't get confused. It will help if you say *you* so that it is really clear that you want your partner to do the steps. Go."

LINK

Before sending children off to write, collect a bunch of things you hope your writers will be keeping in mind as they start new how-to books.

"Remember, whenever you are teaching somebody how to do something, it helps to talk to your readers, using the word *you* so that there isn't any confusion about who you are talking to or what to do for each step. And," I said, pointing to the chart, "you can *always* use this chart as a checklist to help you remember to use everything you know today to make your writing the best it can be. Let me read over our chart, and when I say each item, give me a thumbs up, or a thumbs down, to show if you think are going to do this in your writing today."

> **Learning from a Mentor How-To Text**
>
> 1. The title tells the reader what the book is about
>
> 2. Pictures that teach
>
> 3. List of things you need
>
> 4. Important parts in **bold** or ALL CAPS
>
> 5. Talks to reader (you)

Helping Children Apply and Transfer Strategies for Spelling Trickier Words

AS YOU AND YOUR CHILDREN spend more and more time studying how-to writing, previous units will begin to feel like a distant memory. In the unit prior to this one, you taught them an extensive repertoire of strategies for independently tackling trickier words. You extolled the importance of personal word walls, you coached kids to reread with their "magic pencils" to make sure everything makes sense, and you taught them to listen closely for the vowels in the trickier words. It's perfectly reasonable that these things become less of a focus for students as they learn new things. But it is absolutely important to keep that learning alive for them, and for yourself. Try standing back for the first few minutes of your workshop, observing and researching the whole class, table by table, with a mental checklist (or an actual checklist) of some of your biggest word study goals.

Are children writing trickier words with independence, tackling them with all their strategies, or are they copying words from the word wall and around the room, letter-by-letter, designing their entire piece of writing around the words that happen to be available in the room for correct spelling? (This is more common than you may realize.) The latter is problematic—not only because this is not the most effective way to learn to spell words, but because it is indicative of a much bigger issue. Students working this way are generally not feeling comfortable taking risks. The solution to this problem is *not* to hide all the print! In fact, quite the opposite. You'll need to work hard to create a writing workshop where children are risk takers, where they are not afraid to use words that are tricky to spell, and where they put meaningful work on the page before perfect spelling.

How? Compliment children when they are resourceful and make the attempt to get trickier words down on the page using their best approximations. Seek out examples of children's work that demonstrates a willingness to try and try again—pages where whole sentences have been crossed out, words have been written three times over to try and find the best spelling, where kids tore a whole page out and started fresh again on their own. Stop the class to compliment a tableful of kids who all have their personal word wall words out or to praise the child who circles a tricky word she knows

isn't spelled quite right and just moves on without letting it stop her. These are the signs of a healthy, resilient, confident room full of writers. You will want to make these "old" behaviors just as important to work on as the day's "new" minilesson. If you aren't seeing these behaviors, then you will want to start gathering groups of children to remind them of all the powerful strategies they know and coaching them to practice them all the time, every day, no matter what.

MID-WORKSHOP TEACHING   **Writers Are Resilient and Work to Solve Their Own Problems**

"Eyes on me for a second, everyone. Troyquon just did something so cool that I want to tell you all about. Troyquon's been working so hard today on his how-to book about how to play T-ball. He was so busy adding steps to his book that he kept on adding more and more steps *to the same page*! All of a sudden he took a look at his paper, and what did you realize?"

"It was all squashed up!" Troyquon exclaimed.

"Yup. He was having a hard time rereading it because all of the steps were squashed up together. So what did you do?"

Proudly, Troyquon explained, "I got more pages and fixed it."

"Exactly. Troyquon actually did a couple of smart things. He made sure to reread his work. And when he realized that he needed to add more pages and put a step on each one instead of squashing them all together, he didn't get upset. Nope, not Troyquon! He just hopped up, got more paper, and started to revise. Just like a grown-up writer would do. Hooray for Troyquon! You can all do that, writers. When you realize you need to do a little revision, you can just get to it, on your own, independently, just like Troyquon did."

Noticing More Ways Writers Talk to Their Readers

Choose a favorite page of the class mentor how-to text and read aloud, emphasizing the general playful sound and feel of the language.

"Writers, I noticed so many of you really keeping your readers in mind as you were writing today. Speaking directly to the reader using *you* is a great way to get readers' attention and to make your writing easier to understand. But that's not the only way! Listen to this page and notice how Alyssa Capucilli talks right to us readers. She uses a sort of silly, fun voice, don't you think? When I read her writing, I feel as though I can hear her voice. It's not just a list of steps. Listen.

"I'll just read one or two steps, and your job is to follow along, listening to how Alyssa Satin Capucilli makes it sound like fun." I turned to the middle of one of our favorite parts of the book. "'**Stretch time!** Can you move your knees up and down like a butterfly flutters its wings?'" I paused and looked away from the book. "Wow, it's like she's really talking to us, isn't it! I turned back to the book. "'That's a great **stretch** that will get you warmed up fast! **Hooray!** Now you're ready to **play!**'

"You can write this way too. From now on, don't just list the steps. Really talk to your reader, like you'd talk to a real person—a friend, even."

Today's minilesson introduced a very small, but powerful, strategy for writing with voice and paying attention to language: speaking directly to the reader. I wanted to reinforce the bigger idea of the day's lesson—the language and voice of procedural writing—so I decided to share a few more ways that writers might "talk" to their readers in addition to simply saying "you." I decided to read aloud a few pages from My First Soccer Game, *aiming to highlight the bigger picture, rather than breaking it down into bite-sized strategies.*

FIG. 9–1   This student speaks directly to the reader by using the word *you*, and also by using expressions and wording that he would likely use in conversation such as "BOOM!" and "Power, power up that bat. Pretty goooooood!"

Step 1   First sit on the bench until it is your turn to bat, just in case if it is your first time playing.

Step 2   "Oh no it's going too fast!" When it is your turn to hit the ball this is what the sound makes. BOOM BOOM BOOM BOOM! Don't be scared if it going too fast.

Step 3   "Run!"   When you hit the ball run to 1st base. If somebody catches the ball you're out, but if nobody catches your ball, you're safe. If you're safe, that's good. Make sure you don't miss. To hit a homerun Boom it over the fence. Run the bases. There you score. If you score, that's good. Power, power up that bat. Pretty goooooood!

Step 4   Who get the most points wins. It doesn't matter when you use different counters you worry about winning.

How-To Book Writers Picture Each Step and Then Choose Exactly Right Words

IN THIS SESSION, you'll teach students that writers build vocabulary and choose precise language by envisioning each step in the process they are describing.

GETTING READY

✔ Class-shared writing "How to Make a Peanut Butter and Jelly Sandwich" or whatever text you have been using throughout this unit as your demonstration text (see Connection and Share)

✔ *My First Soccer Game*, by Alyssa Satin Capucilli (see Teaching)

✔ Post-its (see Link and Share)

ADULT READERS AND WRITERS know that one of the most important skills of all is one called "determining importance." The reader of an expository text, for example, is expected to discern "the main idea." And writers are expected to focus, highlighting that which really matters.

As crucial as determining importance is to readers and writers, it is even more critical to teachers, and especially to teachers of young children. After all, you will teach your children tons of things—exposing them to all sorts of lovely, intriguing ideas and possibilities. For example, consider all the marvelous features that children have spotted in the how-to texts they have studied: lists of materials needed, capital letters, bold letters, titles.

Although all of the features kids notice will be cool and exciting (they may discover flaps! or warnings! or exclamation points!), few of these features will have earth-shattering importance. After all, in the sum of things, it is no big deal whether a six-year-old uses bold letters or exclamation points in her writing.

So I want to hasten to say that there absolutely *is* something big that is important about this work, and that is for children to study texts that resemble those they want to write and to resolve to learn from mentor authors, importing techniques those authors have used into their own writing.

This session is an important one. A poet, Grace Paley, once said, "Poetry is the school I went to in order to learn to write prose." Thinking about this, I have come to believe that all kinds of writing have lessons to teach that move beyond a particular genre and apply to all writing. Surely, then, how-to writing is the school that writers go to in order to learn to write clearly, in ways that make sense to readers. In this session we focus on slowing down and picturing the process that's being written about, and on choosing the exactly right words to describe each step in the process. This work is crucial to how-to book writing and is an essential element of any kind of writing.

COMMON CORE STATE STANDARDS: W.K.3, W.K.5, W.K.6, W.K.7, W.1.3, RFS.K.1, RFS.K.2, RFS.K.3, SL.K.1, SL.K.2, SL.K.3, SL.K.6, L.K.1, L.K.2, L.K.5.d, L.K.6

How-To Book Writers Picture Each Step and Then Choose Exactly Right Words

CONNECTION

Remind children that earlier, when they hadn't thought carefully about the steps to follow, they'd produced directions that had not worked.

"Writers, do you remember when we were trying to follow the how-to directions to make a peanut butter and jelly sandwich, and at first the directions said, 'Put the peanut butter on the bread,' so we put the jar of peanut butter on the loaf of bread? Then a minute later the directions said, 'Now eat it,' and we were looking at a tower that had a loaf of bread with two jars on top of it—one of jelly and one of peanut butter? We looked at that tower of stuff and thought, 'Eat it? Are you crazy?'"

"So then we went back and tried to tell more clearly the exact thing that the reader was supposed to do, and we revised it so that it now starts like this (we still need to finish it)."

> How to Make a Peanut Butter and Jelly Sandwich
>
> 1. Get the jar of peanut butter.
>
> 2. Open it, and using your knife, scoop out a knife-full of peanut butter.
>
> 3. Spread the peanut butter over one piece of bread.

"Now our how-to book makes much more sense, and I think, when we finish the book, that we will end up with a real peanut butter and jelly sandwich!"

❖ **Name the teaching point.**

"What I want to teach you today is that to write how-to steps that a reader can easily follow, it is really important to remember yourself doing something and to picture it, almost like you're watching video in slow motion, pausing often to say, 'What exact words describe what I just did?'"

◆ COACHING

The more vividly you can recollect a prior experience, the better the chances your students will understand the connection you are trying to make. In this case, the connection tells a story that sets the purpose for the strategy about to be taught.

TEACHING

Convey to kids that writers work hard to choose the exactly right words to match what they want to say—that precision counts, and leads writers to draft and revise.

"Did you know that when parents are choosing a name for a baby, they often try out about a hundred possible names before choosing one that is exactly right? Like Bradley. Before your parents named you, they probably thought, Fred Morse? Bob Morse? Albert Morse? And only after about a hundred tries did they say, 'Bradley Morse. That's it!'

"I'm telling you this because I can promise you that when Alyssa C. wrote this page about how to kick a soccer ball, she didn't just pick up her pencil and write the words 'Put the ball next to the inside of your foot.'

"She probably first wrote this page like we first wrote about the peanut butter. Remember, it just said, 'Put the peanut butter on the bread'? I bet Alyssa probably first wrote something like 'Kick the soccer ball.'

"Then she probably watched someone else read her book, and they read 'Kick the ball,' so they lifted their leg way up and slammed their heel down on the ball, like this," and I kicked the imaginary ball in a way that sent it flying behind me.

"So let me show you how she probably wrote this page, and you get ready to tell your partner what I am doing (what Alyssa did) that you could try in your writing."

Demonstrate how an author envisions a step in her how-to book and tries out different words until she finds the exactly right ones.

I stood up and put an imaginary soccer ball on the floor. I put my foot beside it (where it goes when making a soccer kick). I muttered, "Go up to the ball and touch it." Then I shook my head, no, and reenacted the action, and this time muttered, "Put your foot beside the ball." I tried again. "Put the ball next to your foot. Put the ball next to the inside of your foot. That's it!" And I started to write that.

ACTIVE ENGAGEMENT

Channel your students to recap your demonstration of picturing a step and choosing the exactly right words.

"Did you see that? Coming up with the exactly right words can take a little work, right? Why don't you turn and talk to you partner about what you saw me doing just now? I didn't just write down any old words. What did I do to help me find the exactly right ones?"

I circulated as the students talked, making mental notes of comments I knew would be helpful to highlight for the whole class.

Of course, don't use the name Bradley if you don't have a Bradley. We recommend you use the name of that one child who keeps you up at night. Make him or her feel famous. This is a variation of the hand on the head, meant to settle the child and to signal, "Stay with me."

Notice that to make a point, we often reach for far-out over-the-top examples that make kids laugh. And remember, be sure when you are saying these words that you are out of the seat, slamming your heel down on that imaginary soccer ball!

After regathering the class, I said, "So, Jeremy, what did you notice?"

"You didn't just write it, you pictured kicking it. So it doesn't go backwards!"

Several other students shared their comments, noticing that I took some time to choose exactly the right words to match the step.

LINK

Rally children to picture each step in the process they are writing about, choosing exactly right words to match.

"So, when you go off to write today, the most important thing to remember is that you want your writing to be easy for other people to understand. You want your readers to be able to do each step exactly the way you picture it. One way to make sure your steps are clear and easy to follow is to picture the step you're writing about and to try out different ways of saying what happens in that step until you find the exactly right words. You can even try different words out by saying them out loud, like I did! If you're revising, you can even cross out old sentences and change them, or add new sentences just like Alyssa might have done in *My First Soccer Game*. There are Post-its in the writing center if you need them!"

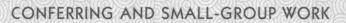

Supporting Students Who Need Extra Help Choosing Exactly Right Words

I HAD A FEW CHILDREN IN MIND to pull for a small group at the beginning of writing time—children who I knew could use some support with choosing more precise and explicit words. I'd included Melanie and Christian, both English language learners, in the group, along with Grace and Jonathan. Gathering the children at the rug, I opened Alyssa's book and explained to the children that sometimes it's really helpful to act out the steps you're trying to write about in addition to picturing the steps in your mind.

"It can really help you find the exactly right words, if you're stuck, because your body gives you ideas as you act it out! Let's try it now with Alyssa's book. Look here. She's writing about how to dribble a soccer ball. Can you try it? Stand up, like you're getting ready to dribble the soccer ball. Don't really run, but kind of act it out in place. As you do that, keep picturing it in your mind as I read the exactly right words Alyssa uses. Ready?" I read from the book. "'Move the ball forward, back, or even side to side!'" Kids giggled as they imagined themselves dribbling the ball and moved their feet accordingly. "Okay. Now picture this. You're going to tap and run. Don't really run! But just move a little bit, to help you get a good picture in your mind. So you're running and dribbling. What would you do next? Kick it hard to pass it? Step on the ball to stop it? You decide what might happen next, and act that out."

I was hoping that using the mentor text, which happened to be about soccer, a familiar game to each of these children, would provide them with a platform to narrow in on more precise language.

"Okay, now, everyone, sit down. We're going to add a new part to Alyssa's book—the part that might come next. Would you guys help me? When you have an idea for the next step in Alyssa's book, give me a thumbs up. What you just did when you were acting it out with your body can help you get ideas." While they were thinking, I asked Grace for her idea. Grace said, "Pass it." The rest of the thumbs were now up.

"Writers, Grace said we could add, 'Pass it,' to the book. We'll add that idea, but first, let's see if we can think of the exactly right words that will help readers know *exactly* what to do. Pass it where? How? Turn and tell your partner."

As kids spoke, I listened in to Christian and Jonathan. "Pass it across the grass," Christian was saying. I wanted Christian to say more, so I whispered to Jonathan, "Ask Christian, 'How do you do that?'"

MID-WORKSHOP TEACHING   **Partners Can Help Each Other Revise for Clarity by Listening to and Acting Out Each Other's Books**

"Writers, I just noticed something George and Erik did that might be helpful for all of you to think about. George was writing along in his book about how to make a sandcastle, and then he got a little stuck. He wasn't sure how to make his steps clearer. He was sitting there, thinking about what might help his writing. Then, listen up. Instead of just thinking about it by himself, he decided to ask Erik, his partner, to try listening to and acting out the steps of George's book.

"When Erik tried to follow the steps, he got confused in some parts, so George told him what to do and then realized the exact words he said needed to go onto the page!

"If you find yourself getting stuck, always remember that you can borrow George and Erik's idea and try reading your writing to a partner."

"How?" Jonathan asked. Christian paused to think. "Umm. Pass it with . . . your foot. It goes on the grass." Although tempted to coach Christian further, I opted to continue. "Christian, you were really thinking about exactly how to do it, weren't you?"

While it may be tempting to coach students to come up with another, close to perfect thing to say, it is not the final sentence that matters most. It's the process of thinking more carefully about what to say and how to say it. If you decide to share a child's idea with the whole class, you can always restate it in a way that clarifies the language and takes it a step further.

"Okay, everyone," I said to the group. "Christian said we could add, 'Use your foot to pass the ball across the grass.'" As I spoke, I wrote this on a Post-it and stuck it into the book. "Those are exactly right words to describe passing a ball. What a great addition to Alyssa's book. I bet you could come up with more things to add, too. Just remember, if you get stuck trying to find exactly right words in your own how-to books, you can always act out what you are picturing. What your body does can help you think of the exactly right words, just like the work we just did with adding on to Alyssa's book."

Writers Practice Picturing a Step and Choosing Exactly Right Words

Referring to both your class text and your mentor text, recall the power of picturing each step and writing the exactly right words.

"Writers, today we remembered that when we worked together on our 'How to Make a Peanut Butter and Jelly Sandwich' directions, we couldn't just write, 'Put on the peanut butter,' or we'd end up with a jar of peanut butter sitting on a loaf of bread! Instead we wrote, 'spread' the peanut butter, right? We learned that how-to book writers try to write clear, specific words that match each step.

"I wonder, for example, what Alyssa might have done when she was trying to teach readers how to dribble a ball. When she was getting ready to write step 1, I bet she closed her eyes and pictured herself getting ready to dribble, and she thought, 'Hmm, where exactly are my feet? Where exactly is the ball?'" I stood up and pretended as though I were Alyssa, with an imaginary soccer ball next to my feet. "She probably pictured the ball in her mind, and she probably said, 'The ball is next to my feet, but wait. There's probably a better way to say it.' I'm sure Alyssa probably said the words a few different ways and finally she wrote, 'Move the ball forward, back, or even side to side! Tap and run. Tap and run.'

"Let's do the same thing now, all together, as we write the end of our how-to book about making a peanut butter and jelly sandwich. Here's what we've got so far."

> How to Make a Peanut Butter and Jelly Sandwich
>
> 1. Get the jar of peanut butter.
>
> 2. Open it, and using your knife, scoop out a knife-full of peanut butter.
>
> 3. Spread the peanut butter over one piece of bread.

"Right here and now, let's picture what we do next. After we spread the peanut butter on, what do we do? Close your eyes and picture it. As you're picturing it, be thinking about the exactly right words to describe what you're picturing. Okay, turn and tell your partner what you might add next, using exactly right words." After listening in for a moment and hearing several ideas, we decided to add, "Open the jelly jar and use your knife to scoop out some jelly."

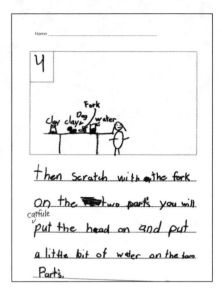

Name Malaya Moore

1

clay   clay and

jentely   Perfect round
First Shape the clay into a ball
to matke the X dog's head

Name

2

clay   head body

jst a lidil
Then take more clay and
shape a body
        dog

Name

3

head
clay | body
      butter

When you are finished
making your head and body
                    small
take a Fork and a boll of
water.

Name

4

Fork
Clay clay Dog water

then scratch with the fork
on the two parts you will
catfule
put the head on and put
a little bit of water on the two
Parts.

Name

5

and do the same and
roll the tail and make
        small   blak and white
the eares and paint it
and put it in the ofan for a
Hour

FIG. 10–1   Encourage children to try the strategy many times, rather than just once. Malaya has inserted better, more exact words throughout her piece.

The book now looked like this.

> How to Make a Peanut Butter and Jelly Sandwich
>
> 1. Get the jar of peanut butter.
>
> 2. Open it, and using your knife, scoop out a knife-full of peanut butter.
>
> 3. Spread the peanut butter over one piece of bread.
>
> 4. Open the jelly jar and use your knife to scoop out some jelly.

"Yep, I think those are exactly the right words to help readers know how to do the next step! Now you can try it in your own writing! Right now, reread your writing and find a place where *you* worked really hard to write with the exactly right words, and you can leave a celebration Post-it on that page. You will need to decide what goes on your celebration Post-it. Balloons? Fireworks? A picture of Superman? That is up to you. But be sure to find a place where you worked hard to make the words exactly right."

Elaboration in How-To Books

Writers Guide Readers with Warnings,
Suggestions, and Tips

IN THIS SESSION, you'll teach students that writers focus on readers' needs by anticipating issues and then clarifying them in their steps with warnings, suggestions, or tips.

GETTING READY

✔ Prepare a "real-life" story of how a friend got helpful warnings and tips when she was learning to do something (see Connection)

✔ *My First Soccer Game* by Alyssa Satin Capucilli (see Teaching)

✔ Enlarged version of class text, "How to Make a Peanut Butter and Jelly Sandwich" (see Active Engagement)

✔ A jar of peanut butter and a knife that you will use to demonstrate the first few steps of your class text (see Active Engagement)

✔ "Learning from a Mentor How-To Text" chart (see Active Engagement)

✔ Chart paper and marker (see Share)

✔ Work from a few children who have incorporated the language of a warning, suggestion, or tip in their writing (see Share)

COMMON CORE STATE STANDARDS: W.K.2, W.K.5, W.1.2, RI.K.1, RI.K.2, SL.K.1, SL.K.2, L.K.1, L.K.2, L.K.6, L.1.1.j

E LABORATION IS AN IMPORTANT PART of any informational text. All-about books elaborate with examples, descriptions, and anecdotes. Procedural texts are different. The actual steps tend to be lean, often written in the brief language of commands. "Turn the oven to 350 degrees. Get out eggs, milk, a bowl, and a large spoon." The whole point is to coach the reader along through a progression of activities, and to do so as efficiently as possible.

There are important ways, however, that authors of how-to texts do elaborate. When children learn them, they can write more, and that, of course, means they are spelling more, using high-frequency words more, rereading more, and doing all this with greater fluency. Speed and automaticity in writing matter a lot because it is only when one can write quickly that writing can really function as an important tool for learning across every discipline. That is crucially important in any effort to create mindful learning.

Elaboration matters in how-to books also because writers say more as a result of thinking carefully about the reader and working to supply the reader with all that he or she will need to successfully follow the directions.

Finally, the strategies that you will teach today matter because the effort to do this sort of elaboration can lead children toward understanding the complex relationships between the main message of a text and the messages contained in its peripheral features.

And so today you will teach children to include cautionary notes and extra tips in their how-to books. They will be doing what teachers, parents, and caregivers often do, as people who are adept at considering their audience. Today, then, you teach kids how to think more about their audience, the way teachers think about their classrooms, anticipating the kinds of tips and warnings that might be helpful.

For kindergartners, life is filled with warnings, cautions, and tips. This lesson is a favorite among kids. It is fun, after all, to teach well and be understood.

Elaboration in How-To Books
Writers Guide Readers with Warnings, Suggestions, and Tips

CONNECTION

Tell a story from real life about a time when warnings and tips helped a learner avoid mishap.

"Writers, last week my six-year-old friend Madison got her first bicycle for her birthday. She was so excited. Her mom and I took her outside for her first ride. She had never ridden a bike before.

"She wheeled the bike out to the sidewalk, put her helmet loosely on, and started to climb up onto the seat when a neighbor, Mr. Roy, came by. 'I got a new bike! I'm gonna learn how to ride!' she said.

"Mr. Roy said, 'That's exciting! But you know, with those shorts on, if you fall, you are going to skin your knees and it will hurt. You should put on long pants!'

"With a nod from her mom, Madison disappeared into the house, and three minutes later, she was back on the sidewalk wearing jeans, her helmet still cockeyed on her head. Another neighbor, Mrs. Marconi, came walking by. 'Look at you, Madison! A new bike! But you aren't going to learn to ride on a sidewalk, are you? It is too narrow and bumpy,' Mrs. Marconi said. 'Why don't you go over to the empty parking lot by the school. Schools are closed on Sunday and no cars will come in the parking lot.' Wow! What great advice!

"We started heading to the school when Mrs. Marconi caught up to us and added another note. 'And that helmet looks like it is about to fall off. Tighten the strap!'

"Madison's mom and I were so glad we got all those warnings and tips. Can you imagine if Madison's helmet fell off while she was riding her bike for the first time? Or if she wore shorts and then fell?"

❧ Name the teaching point.

"Today I want to teach you that in how-to books, writers don't just teach the steps. They also add little warnings and tips. They do this by thinking about how the learner could go wrong and then adding advice to keep that from happening."

As you prepare for this lesson, think of times from your own life when a warning or a tip helped you avoid a mishap. Then substitute that story for this one.

When using an anecdote like this from real life, tell it in a memorable, engaging way. Use characters' names, put in dialogue, and tell it expressively. Dramatize as much as possible.

TEACHING

Reading aloud a mentor text, ask children to notice when they hear warnings or tips.

"Let me read you a few pages from *My First Soccer Game*. Put your thumbs up if you hear Alyssa Capucilli giving advice, suggestions, or warnings like Madison's neighbors were giving her." I read the text, and when I came to a warning, I shook my finger at the class to accentuate that this was serious advice.

> *It doesn't matter if you're big or small!* <u>*Don't forget! In soccer you don't use your hands!*</u>

The children giggled at my exaggerated gesture, and thumbs popped up around the room.

I continued reading. "Let's listen for other warnings or tips that Alyssa gives. If you hear one of those warnings or tips, use your finger," and I shook my index finger," to accompany that warning." I read on.

> *Pass the ball back and forth to a teammate as you run. That's called passing.* <u>*Be sure to practice with both feet!*</u>

As I came to the warning, the kindergartners delightedly admonished me and each other, shaking their fingers with gusto.

ACTIVE ENGAGEMENT

Suggest that students add similar warning and tips to a class text. As the text is read aloud, recruit children to imagine possible mishaps and suggest cautionary notes.

"You're noticing so many places in her book about how to play soccer where Alyssa is giving readers little tips and warnings. You know what? I bet you could add warnings and tips to our how-to book about making a peanut butter and jelly sandwich! Let's try it. Let's go back now and put in a few warnings, tips, or suggestions.

"I am going to ask Rebecca to read 'How to Make a Peanut Butter and Jelly Sandwich' out loud while I try to follow our directions. Pay close attention, because things might go wrong! I'm going to ask you to come up with warnings or tips to keep readers on track."

Rebecca read aloud, "Step 1. Get the jar of peanut butter."

I picked the jar up off the desk where I had placed the peanut butter, smiled confidently at the class, and then halfway back to my seat I suddenly dropped the jar on the floor. I looked at the class in shock. Giggles erupted. Then I reached for a knife that was on the floor, wiped it semi-clean, and stuck it into the peanut butter jar.

It's not necessary to read the entire text in a minilesson. Just an example or two will usually do. Remember, mentor texts for writing are already familiar texts.

Dramatizing what could happen without the new strategy applied to the writing helps students understand why today's lesson is so important.

Ask students to turn and talk to their partners, sharing warnings or tips that might help how-to book readers avoid mishaps.

"Okay, writers, what did you notice? Tell your partners what warnings or tips we could give readers of our how-to book to keep things from going wrong."

As I moved around the room listening in, I smiled to see many children using an admonishing index finger as they shared tips and warnings to add to our book. Gathering the class, I highlighted a few. "I'm hearing some great suggestions, writers. Melissa says that she wants to add, 'Be careful that you don't drop the jar.' And Damien thinks that 'Be sure that the knife is clean,' would be a good tip. Great work!" I added these warnings in, quickly. The book now read:

How to Make a Peanut Butter and Jelly Sandwich

1. Get the jar of peanut butter. *Be careful that you don't drop the jar.*
2. Open it, and using your knife, scoop out a knife-full of peanut butter. *Be sure the knife is clean.*
3. Spread the peanut butter over one piece of bread.
4. Open the jelly jar and use your knife to scoop out some jelly.

"Also, I'm going to add 'warnings, suggestions, and tips' to our 'Learning from a Mentor How-To Text' chart, because how-to writing is always stronger when authors imagine what might go wrong for readers and then give them tips so they don't have those problems!"

Learning from a Mentor
How-To Text

1. The title tells the reader what the book is about

2. Pictures that teach

3. List of things you need

4. Important parts in **bold** or ALL CAPS

5. Talks to reader (you)

6. Warnings, suggestions, and tips

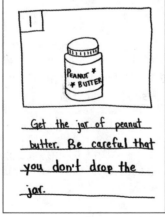

FIG. 11–1   The class how-to continues to grow over time.

LINK

As you send children off to continue working on their how-to books, remind them to help readers avoid mishaps by adding helpful warnings and tips.

"So, writers, as you start working today, remember that you can be the kind of writers who give helpful advice to your readers. When you write warnings and tips, you are helping your readers better understand your directions, and you're helping them avoid the kinds of problems they might have otherwise. Today you might start by adding warnings or tips to the how-to book you are working on now, and then you might decide to go back and revise how-to books you have already written by adding those things in."

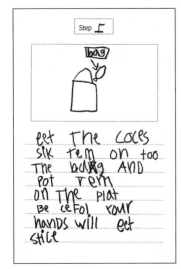

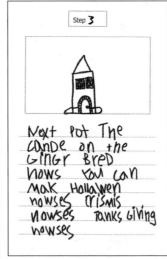

Step 1   Get the cookies. Stick them onto the bag and put them on the plate. Be careful, your hands will get sticky.

Step 2   Then put the icing on so the candy can stick. Put enough icing because you want to put lots of candy on.

Step 3   Next put the candy on the gingerbread house. You can make Halloween houses, Christmas house, [and/or] Thanksgiving houses.

Step 4   Then wrap the plastic paper around the gingerbread house so it can't fall.

Step 5   Finally, tie it with ribbon so it can't fall out once more.

FIG. 11–2   This student's writing about how to make a gingerbread house is sprinkled with cautions such as "Be careful, your hands will get sticky," and tips like "Put enough icing because you want to put lots of candy on." Notice how she also makes use of previously taught strategies such as labels, using *you* to speak directly to the reader, and transition words (*first, then, next, finally*).

Coaching Students to Use Many Revision Strategies, Not Just One

A S I SAT DOWN BETWEEN JULISSA AND GRACE, I could tell that both girls had taken the minilesson to heart, which was typical for these students. They were both busily adding dramatic cautionary notes to their how-to books. The girls often worked in tandem, and in this case, it seemed to be working nicely for them. They were sharing words and phrases with each other and giggling softly. As I looked at Julissa's paper, I noticed that she'd run out of room for her warning, "Be careful, the stove is hot!" and had started writing it up the side of her paper. Grace was doing something similar.

I had a couple of things in mind to teach them. I wanted to remind them of a revision method we'd discovered earlier in the year—cutting and taping a strip of paper to a book so that there's more room to add on. But I also wanted to extend and unfold that work a little bit. The process of revision is not just about adding a strip of paper, obviously. And there are more ways to revise a piece than to just add on the warnings and cautionary notes we'd discussed in the minilesson.

I decided to extend the girls' thinking about their revision work. It's not just about sticking on a couple of warnings in one piece and being done for the day! I complimented them on the fact that they'd both added on warnings and reminded them that when they run out of space like that they can always make a strip of paper to add on their revision so it's easier to read. Then I said, "You know, girls, you both have a whole stack of how-to books that you've written. Instead of just focusing on adding warnings to one book, writers actually can go through a whole stack of books and make revisions in each of them—revisions that make sense for each book. You might add warnings, like you did in the books you're working on now, but you might instead make sure your books have titles or see if there's a really exciting place where it makes sense to add all caps or bold. You know lots of ways to revise. So instead of focusing on just one way to revise in just one book, your work for today might be to go through four or five books and do some quick revision work in each of them. And remember, you can always add a strip if you run out of space!"

I definitely wanted to support the fact that Julissa and Grace were trying out what was suggested in the minilesson, but I also wanted to pull out a larger point. Our conferences and small groups are most effective when they do not simply mirror the minilesson, but meet students where they are and boost them up to a new level, based on what they are actually doing when we approach. I knew that Julissa and Grace were ready to think about the bigger picture of revision work.

MID-WORKSHOP TEACHING
Adding Advice and Warnings for Your Reader

"Writers, eyes on me for a sec. I want to share with you something I just heard in a conversation between Damien and William. Damien was asking William what kind of suggestions he could add to his book 'How to Go Skateboarding.' William said, 'Just write down something like what your mom would say.' This is a great idea, William!

"I'm sure that many of you know grown-ups who give you advice and warnings all the time. Thumbs up if anyone has ever said this to you on a cold day: 'Make sure you wear your hat or you might get sick.'" Thumbs and grins popped up across the room. "And thumbs up if anybody has ever told you, 'If you want to be healthy, you must eat your vegetables.'" Lots more thumbs and grins. "Grown-ups give advice all the time. When you are adding advice to your how-to books, one way to think about what to write is to make believe that there is a grown-up there, whispering in your ear.

"Those grown-up warnings about what you should and shouldn't do are the kinds of things you can tell your readers to help them understand your directions perfectly and to keep things from going wrong."

Writers Use Particular Words to Convey Warnings, Suggestions, or Tips

Draw students' attention to particular words that convey warnings, suggestions, or tips, and begin a chart to collect words students notice.

After convening the children with their writing folders in the meeting area, I said, "I noticed so many of you adding warnings and tips to your how-to books today! You are sure saving your readers some trouble! You know what else I noticed? Some of you have been using certain words when you give warnings, suggestions, and tips. These words help readers know what's coming. Let's make a quick list of some of these words. I'm going to say some of the warning, suggestion, or tip words I have seen in your books, and if you are one of the writers who has used those words, please read that sentence in your book."

I wrote, "Warnings, Suggestions, and Tips" at the top of a piece of paper. Then I said, "Okay, first example: Be careful!" I wrote, "Be careful." "I know at least one of you has included those words in your book. Rachel, you did, didn't you? Can you read your book to us?" Rachel pulled her piece out and read.

How to Make an Ice Cream–by Rachel

You Need

Vanilla Ice Cream, Cone, Scooper, Sprinkles

First you get the ice-cream. Be careful. Do not drop it.

Next you get the scooper. And make sure the scooper is clean.

Then you get the cone. You get the cone from freezer. And you get the scooper. Make sure it's clean.

Then you put some frosting on. You get it outside.

Last you eat it. Yummy!

"Thumbs up if you used the words *be careful* today." A couple of students raised their thumbs. "Okay, next one: watch out." Elisabet's hand waved wildly. "Yep, Elisabet, I thought you'd used *watch out*! Will you read that part of your book to us, please?"

① HOW TO Make an ice-cream cone. BY _____

② Ice-cream YOU NEED Cone Scooper | Vanilla Ice-cream | Sprinkels | Sprinkels

③ Strawberry ice-cream. First you get the ice-cream Be careful do not drop it

④ Next you get the scooper And make sure the scooper is clean

⑤ Then, you get the cone. You get the cone from the freezer And you get the scooper. Make Sure its clean.

⑥ Then you put some frosten on You get it outside.

⑦ Yummy Last you eat it Yummy!

FIG. 11–3   Rachel gives advice and suggestions on making an ice cream cone.

Elisabet read, "Take the toast out of the toaster. Watch out so you don't burn your fingers!"

"Thumbs up if you used those words today." More thumbs. We went through the same quick process with the words *I suggest* and *don't*. I added the names of the children who'd shared their examples next to the words on the chart, making a note to photocopy those pages from their books to add on later as well.

Before wrapping up, I said, "You're all discovering lots of helpful words to use when you're writing warnings, suggestions, and tips so that readers know what's coming. I'd love to know if you come up with something that we don't have up here yet so we can add it to the list later."

I made a note to myself to follow up and add new ideas to the list during morning meeting or some other time during the day.

"Balance on One Leg Like a Flamingo"

Using Comparisons to Give Readers Clear Directions

IN THIS SESSION, you'll teach students that writers clarify their directions by imagining and then writing comparisons to describe actions.

GETTING READY

✔ "Learning from a Mentor How-To Text" chart (see Connection and Share)

✔ Children's writing folders (see Connection, Active Engagement, and Share)

✔ *My First Soccer Game* by Alyssa Satin Capucilli (see Teaching)

✔ Post-its (see Share)

✔ An exemplary piece of student writing (see Share)

INFORMATIONAL TEXTS, like the how-to books your students are writing, are not by definition dry and dull. Quite the opposite, in fact! The most engaging and effective informational writing can be as thrilling as an action movie. Teaching your students crafting techniques that can be used across genres will enrich the work they are doing in this unit and will carry through into the writing they do from here on out. Writing similes and metaphors (for our youngest writers, here, we simplify and call them *comparisons*) is one way to bring any writing into living color. In the context of how-to books, not only will teaching children to incorporate comparisons into their writing liven up their writing, bring a sense of fun and playfulness, and deepen their envisioning skills as they write, but writing comparisons is also an important and effective way to make directions as clear and explicit as possible. The directions "Stand on one leg" do provide some information for the reader, but including the comparison "Stand on one leg *like a flamingo*" adds so much more, in terms of both clarity and resonance. The reader who can envision a flamingo standing tall and straight, one leg lifted up, perfectly balanced, will bring that image to mind when envisioning herself getting ready to kick a soccer ball—balanced, straight, ready.

You may be tempted to think of this lesson as "just for fun." And it is fun! It is fun to help your students start thinking metaphorically in the context of their how-to directions. They will love acting out comparisons, and they will love thinking of them. But thinking metaphorically is so much more than just fun. In this context, it provides another way for children to think through their directions and make sure they are as clear as possible for their readers. And metaphor is at the root of so much great literature and thinking. This is the very beginning of a lifetime journey exploring, enjoying, and creating comparisons to better understand and describe the world.

COMMON CORE STATE STANDARDS: W.K.2, W.K.5, RI.K.1, SL.K.1, L.K.1, L.K.2, L.K.5

"Balance on One Leg Like a Flamingo"

Using Comparisons to Give Readers Clear Directions

CONNECTION

Recap and celebrate all that children have learned so far.

"I was thinking back to when we first began writing how-to books and you were all sitting in our meeting area just like you are now. Only then, many of you did not even realize what a how-to book sounded like. I know that some of you did not even know how to write steps and clear directions. Hard to believe, right? I think before we go any further you all need to congratulate yourself on all of the new things you've learned to do as writers. Will you open your folders now and get an example of your best how-to book and put a thumb up when you have it?" The children shuffled through their folders and put proud thumbs in the air.

"Great, writers. Can I have all eyes up here? Let's look at our chart."

Using the anchor chart as part of the minilesson helps to keep it fresh on children's minds and encourages them to refer to it as they work.

Learning from a Mentor How-To Text

1. The title tells the reader what the book is about

2. Pictures that teach

3. List of things you need

4. Important parts in **bold** or ALL CAPS

5. Talks to reader (you)

6. Warnings, suggestions, and tips

Find every opportunity you can to remind children to use all the strategies you've taught so far, not just one from day's minilesson.

"Writers, I am going to read this chart about what makes a how-to book. Look at your best how-to book as I read. When you hear something that you think you have done in your book, stand up and take a bow. Okay, number 1, 'The title tells the reader what the book is about.'" Five beaming writers took their bows. "Next, 'Pictures that teach . . .'" I continued to read through the list until every member of the class had taken a bow. "Congratulations, writers! I can see that you are all becoming experts on how to write a how-to book! Do you think some of you are ready for a new challenge?" Writers nodded their heads emphatically.

✤ Name the teaching point.

"Today I want to teach you another way to show readers exactly what you mean for them to do when they read your how-to directions. It's called *making comparisons*."

TEACHING

Ask volunteers to follow your directions. Alternate giving a stark command with a direction that explains *how* to do that same thing, using the word *like* and a comparison. Contrasting directions should highlight the value of comparisons.

"First, I need four volunteers to come up here." I quickly collected four of my more wiggly children. "I'm going to give you some directions, and your job is to follow my directions. Some will be easy to follow, some will be hard, and later we will talk about the difference. Ready?"

"Try this: *Line up.*" The students got into a rough line.

"Now try *this*! Line up *like* you're a freight train! The person in the front is the engine! The rest of you are the cars!"

Automatically, the students attached themselves like train cars. I even heard some train sounds coming from somewhere in the line.

"Great. Now, *march in place.*" There was some halfhearted marching.

"Now. March *like* a family of penguins!" This produced a grinning, bobbing row of waddling marchers.

"*Stand up and sit down.*"

"Now, listen carefully, because this will be hard: Stand up and sit down *like* . . ." I left a bit of space in hopes the children would be generating their own options. "Are you thinking of what we could compare this to?" I asked before continuing. "Stand up and sit down like you are a yo-yo on the end of a string!"

Now give the whole class the same experience.

This time I signaled that the volunteers could sit down, and I said to the whole class, "Will you all be volunteers?" They nodded. "Try this: Put your two hands together." Then, waiting just long enough to create a drumroll, I said, "Now put your hands together *like* you are clapping because your team just won the World Series."

Any time you can get kids moving is sure to make for a more memorable and engaging lesson!

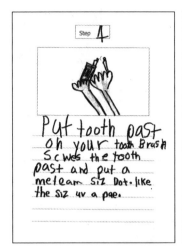    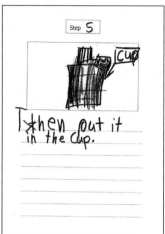

Step 1   Put toothpaste on your toothbrush. Squeeze the tooth-paste and put a medium size dot, like the size of a pea.

Step 2   Put water on your toothbrush. Don't put really hot water or your teeth will burn.

Step 3   Scrub your teeth soft like a tickle.

Step 4   Then wash it when you're done.

Step 5   Then put it in the cup.

FIG. 12–1   This student tries out comparisons in her writing. Comparisons help the reader understand her directions.

Debrief, revving kids up with compliments. Show that their mentor author uses this technique, and so can they.

"Let me show you how Alyssa Capucilli uses comparisons. Listen and act out her steps with me. Stand up for this one. Are you ready?

"Lift your knees high, like you're marching in a parade." The kids marched, smiling, and I coached into it. "Yes, see? You guys are great at comparisons! You are really marching just like you were in a parade!

"Now try this one from Alyssa Capucilli. 'Can you balance on one leg . . . like a flamingo?' Another comparison! Great work kindergartners. You're doing it! All you have to do is think, 'What is this like?' and use your special kid-powers to help you pretend a little bit when you want to make a comparison."

ACTIVE ENGAGEMENT

Guide students to come up with a comparison for one of the steps in their how-to books.

"I know you cannot wait to try this! It's fun, isn't it? Open one of your books—any one of them—to a page where you are telling your reader what to do. When you act out the step, think to yourself, 'What is this like? What does it remind me of?' Maybe you will need to pretend a little bit. Then just pick up your pen and add a comparison. Sometimes just writing the word *like* will help you get started."

After a few moments, I said, "Now get help from your partner and see if you can come up with a way to finish that comparison. Like . . . what? If you think of something, tell your partner."

LINK

Encourage students to add comparisons to the collection of things they know how to incorporate into writing how-to books.

"Writers, today you learned one more thing you can do to make your how-to books even clearer, to make it even easier for readers to follow what you are saying. Writers, tomorrow is our last day in this bend of the road of our unit, and by tomorrow many of you will have written at least ten how-to books. I am pretty sure that some of you will decide to start another new how-to book today, making it your very, very best because you are going to have time tomorrow to choose your best how-to book and to do something special with it.

"Some of you, however, need to finish your last how-to book instead of starting a new one. You will need to decide.

"Writers, you have a lot of ways that you can help your reader learn your topic. In each and every how-to book you write, you have decisions to make. Ask yourself, what else should I add that can make my steps even clearer? If you are going to make a diagram, where are you going to do that? If you are going to make a comparison, where are you going to add that? Writers have important decisions to make each and every day."

It is important when we send students off to write that we are not giving them an "assignment" but instead a list of options for their independent work time. However, with subtleties of language, we can nudge them toward work that we think is important for them to do.

Gathering a Group of Writers with Similar Needs

AS I PULLED UP TO LEXI and noticed that she could use some support adding comparisons to her how-to book, I decided to jump on the opportunity to work on this with Troyquon and Sofia as well.

"Lexi, let's get a team of writers together to think about this. Will you go tap Troyquon and Sofia on the shoulders and meet me on the rug with your writing folders?" As the children settled in, I said, "Writers, I asked Lexi if I could borrow her book—'How to Take Care of My Dog.' She's working on adding some comparisons, and she's a little stuck. I thought we might all put our heads together and help her out, and then you three can talk about adding comparisons to Troyquon and Sofia's how-to books as well. So, Lexi, read your book to us. We'll all be thinking about places where you might add comparisons." Lexi began to read.

"Now, let's chat about ideas you might have for Lexi. Is there a place where she could add a comparison to help readers picture exactly what she means?" Silence. I could tell the group would need a bit more scaffolding. I grabbed *My First Soccer Game*. "Remember how Alyssa used comparisons to help us picture exactly what we were supposed to do? She didn't just write, 'Lift your knees high.' She wrote, 'Lift your knees high like you're marching in a parade!' How does that help us picture that step more clearly?"

Troyquon jumped up and said, "In parades, they go like this!" He demonstrated some vigorous high-knee marching. I motioned for him to sit down, and said, "Exactly! Because you have a picture in your mind already of how people march in a parade, it helps you picture what Alyssa means by lift your knees high. I wonder about the steps in Lexi's book. 'Mix it carefully.' Hmm, you mean the dog food, right, Lexi? Guys, what could Lexi compare mixing up dog food carefully to?"

"You mix it carefully . . . like . . . holding a baby!" Jaqui said. "Oh, wow! You really do need to hold babies carefully, that's true! Do you want to add that, Lexi?" Of course, stirring dog food as carefully as holding a baby is a little over-the-top, but I wanted to support all the gestures kids made toward using comparisons at this point, as long as they made sense.

After taking more suggestions from her classmates and thinking of some on her own, Lexi had plenty of ideas to add. I set Troyquon and Sofia up to help each other in a similar fashion before I got up to work with other writers.

Note that conferences and small groups do not always or even often line up so precisely with the minilesson topic. In this case, I wanted to jump on the comparison energy in the room and help these three students practice adding comparisons in a concrete way while the idea was still fresh in their minds.

MID-WORKSHOP TEACHING
Writers Can Use New Strategies to Revise Old Work

"Writers, I want to remind you that you can also go back through your folder and find some of your favorite how-to booklets that you wrote a while ago and revise them. That means working on how-to books that are in the 'Finished' side of your folder. There are books you haven't looked at in a while, and you have learned so many new things since then. You might find some old books that you can make much better by revising using some of your newest learning."

As Students Continue Working . . .

"You'll know that you are finished with a piece, finished for good, when you've decided whether you want to add everything on your 'How-To Book' charts!"

"If you don't think you want something in your how-to book, like a warning or bold words, that's your decision. You are the boss of your writing."

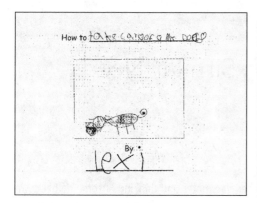

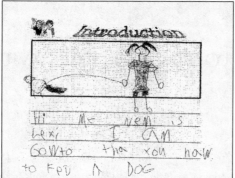

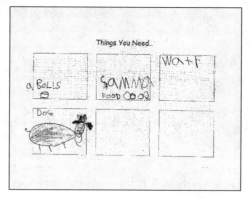

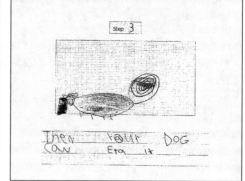

Step 1–Get your dog. Then pour the food in the dog's bowl.

Step 2–Next. Put some water in the food bowl. Then mix it carefully.

Step 3–Then your dog can eat it.

Step 4–Good job you can do it!

Step 5–I know you could do it!

FIG 12–2   Students offer suggestions to Lexi on places in her writing where she might add comparisons.

Writers Celebrate all They've Learned from Mentor Authors

Highlight a student who has borrowed a strategy from a mentor author.

I asked the children to come to the rug with their writing folders with a pen tucked inside and to sit on them so they wouldn't be distracted as I began. They sat next to their writing partners.

"I just have to share with you how Chloe tried out comparisons in her writing today. Listen to this." I read from Chloe's writing, putting special emphasis on the parts where she used comparisons.

"Writers, how many of you tried today's strategy of adding comparisons, like Chloe did? Thumbs up if you tried it." Many thumbs went up. "Excellent. How many of you think you might try it tomorrow?" More thumbs went up.

"Writers, we've been spending lots of time with this great book, *My First Soccer Game* by Alyssa Satin Capucilli. She feels like a good friend now, doesn't she? We've learned so much from studying her writing. Let's celebrate! First, let's read our chart together. Join in with me. And if you tried out the things we're reading about, give yourself a pat on the back!"

First you buy balloons, presents, and cards.

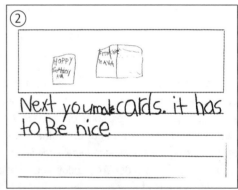

Next you make cards. It has to be nice.

Then you blow up the balloon so it's round and shiny like the sun.

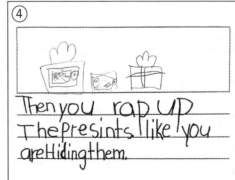

Then you wrap up the presents like you are hiding them.

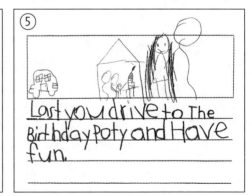

Last you drive to the birthday party and have fun.

FIG. 12–3 Chloe uses comparisons in her writing.

We did a shared reading of the now-familiar chart, and the rug was of course filled with enthusiastic back-patters.

Learning from a Mentor How-To Text

1. The title tells the reader what the book is about

2. Pictures that teach

3. List of things you need

4. Important parts in **bold** or CAPS

5. Talks to reader (you)

6. Warnings, suggestions, and tips

7. Comparisons

"I know that you've discovered other great things to try out in your how-to books from studying the work of other authors—both the books we find in libraries and books written by your own classmates! Some of you have tried out adding a flap or a text box. Some of you have added exclamation points to really exciting parts. And this isn't the end of that work! Writers *always* study each other's work and learn new things to try out. So today we're going to celebrate all of that hard work. Remember a while ago when you put a celebration Post-it on a place in your book where you wrote with exactly right words? Well, today, you'll choose the book that you've been working the hardest on lately. Maybe you tried out lots of new things you've learned from Alyssa and other writers. And I'm going to give you a celebration Post-it to put right on the front page! You can draw or write on the Post-it. When you're done, you can read your books to your partners!"

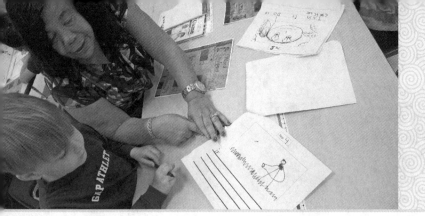

Writers Write How-To Books about Things They Learn throughout the Day and from Books

IN THIS SESSION, you'll teach students that writers get ideas for their writing from things that they do and learn throughout the day and from books.

GETTING READY

✔ A Museum of the School Year table, set up with artifacts from across the children's school day, organized into baskets for each table for easy management (see Connection, Teaching, and Active Engagement)

✔ A basketball, borrowed from the P.E. teacher (see Connection)

✔ Find a writer who has written two or three books on a similar topic in preparation for the next day's minilesson (see Session 14).

UNTIL NOW, this unit has drawn from your children's extensive knowledge of how to do things outside school like riding scooters, changing their baby sister's diaper, cooking French toast. Now you will ask them to think across *more* of their lives to uncover whole areas of expertise about school that they may not have realized they could teach others. This part of the unit presents an opportunity for them to articulate and to teach others things they know how to do during reading, writing, science, math, and so forth.

Of course, the actual work children will be doing won't be any different than what they have been doing all along. The subject matter will change a bit, but they'll still be drawing on all they have come to know about this genre of writing and about writing in ways that allow them to teach readers to do things. Don't feel bad that this final bend revisits previous learning. The truth is that until now, you have not exactly followed the cooking directions—"add flour slowly, stirring all the while." You have dumped a lot of new strategies and new concepts on very young learners, so giving your children time to draw from all they know, transferring all that you have taught them to this new forum, is probably the best thing you could do for your kids.

But you will want to make them feel as if this is very new and exciting work. Prior to teaching this session, you may want to gather up some artifacts from across various portions of the children's school day for a Classroom Museum that can jog their memories of things they have learned to do in school. The art and P.E. teachers can contribute, and children can collect artifacts that represent their school knowledge—old reading and writing workshop charts, items from experiments and art projects, and the like—but don't tell them why until you explain the plan for this final portion of the unit.

COMMON CORE STATE STANDARDS: W.K.2, W.K.8, W.1.7, RI.K.1, SL.K.1, SL.K.4, L.K.1, L.K.2, L.K.6

Writers Write How-To Books about Things They Learn throughout the Day and from Books

CONNECTION

Draw students' attention to artifacts you've collected, suggesting that these artifacts can help them think of how-to book topics.

"Writers, I know some of you have been noticing that a couple of kids and I have been gathering things that represent all you have done this year. On the table, we have set up what I think could be called a Museum of the School Year. And I am hoping that the things on the table—and the things you could put on your very own museum table—represent things that some of you have learned how to do this year in school. Let's see if this works. I will pick up an item, and you can think, 'Does that item get me thinking of something that I know how to do, something I could teach others?' You ready?"

I walked to the table, picked up and bounced a basketball, and said, "I heard that some of you know how to dribble and some of you know how to shoot for a basket. If this ball makes you think of something you know how to do, stand up and take a bow."

Five kids jumped to their feet, and as they bowed I said, "You know, the funny thing is, I have not yet seen any books from this class called 'How to Play Basketball' or 'How to Shoot Hoops' or 'How to Dribble a Ball.' What's up with that?" The class giggled.

"Writers, I'm talking to you about this because I am thinking that in the next bend in the road of this unit, you should make a pact to be sure that all your how-to books teach people about things you have learned in school and from books."

❖ Name the teaching point.

"Today I want to teach you that *all of you*, every single one of you, has learned to do things at school, as well as at home. You can even write how-to books that help others learn something that you *just* learned in school yesterday! And there are lots of objects in school that can remind you of how-to books you could write."

It is important that children remember that how-to books are teaching books, and everything they have learned this year is a potential topic. Everything from how to line up in the cafeteria to how to build a bridge in the block center makes for a wonderful teaching book.

We can help children see that any artifact in the museum can yield several topics. The basketball may not only yield "How to Shoot Hoops" or "How to Dribble a Ball," but can also yield "How to Put Away the Equipment We Use at Recess."

TEACHING

Demonstrate how you can use an artifact from school to get ideas for your next how-to book.

"Remember that if you need help coming up with how-to books, you can look at our Museum of the School Year (or start making your own Museum of the School Year), letting objects in the museum spark ideas in your mind. Let's try it. Take a look at this baggie of leaves. Does it remind you of something?" Kids' hands shot up as they called out "The leaf study!"

"Here is the hard question, though. What did we learn to *do* that we could write about in a how-to book? Hmm. Oh, I know one thing! We learned how to draw a leaf. Remember we used a magnifying glass? Let's see if we can remember the steps." I paused and made an exaggerated expression to show that I was thinking hard about this.

"Step 1: hold the magnifying glass up to the leaf." I held up one finger for each step of my how-to book. "Step 2: look very closely at one part of the leaf. Step 3: draw exactly what you see. Do you see, writers, that first you look at something and let it spark an idea about something you learned to do? Then you think about the steps, listing them across your fingers like you always do when writing a how-to book. And pretty soon I better sketch the steps before I forget how the book will go."

FIG. 13–1 A classroom museum can be as simple as a table like this one, displaying favorite books, shared writing, and activities from across the school year.

ACTIVE ENGAGEMENT

Organize students to examine artifacts, using them to spark memories of things they've learned how to do.

"Okay, now it's your turn to get ideas for your next how-to books by thinking of what you have learned to do in school. Let's let the first row of kids go over to the museum and see if one of those objects sparks an idea. While they are on their way, the rest of you can think about what objects you would put in your very own museum, one that has the things you are most interested in. And tell each other what item you might put in your museum and what memories it sparks for something you know how to do.

"Writers, how many of you now have an idea for a how-to book you can write that teaches people how to do something you have learned in school? How to write a story. How to make a collage. How to make a leaf collection. How to choose a just-right book. Thumbs up if you have an idea for a how-to book you will write."

LINK

Channel students to list the steps of their how-to book topics across their fingers.

"Now, writers, the hard part. Think what the steps are, and list them across your fingers. Do that by yourself, and when I see that you are coming up with the steps, I'll tap you on the shoulder, and you can go and get started."

When you confer today, be on the lookout for a student who has written or is writing more than one book about the same topic. If no one has done this, you can coach into it. You'll need examples for tomorrow's minilesson.

Coaching Conferences

THERE ARE TWO SIDES OF THE COIN to today's lesson. On the one hand, this lesson is designed to help kids conjure up even more ideas for possible how-to books. On the other hand, when children are writing about content areas, vocabulary might be more challenging. Some of your children may need support with the language for talking about and writing the steps for how to do the less familiar things they've most recently learned to do in school. When helping children to go from looking at an artifact and remembering things they have done to orienting themselves in a fashion that will produce a procedural text, part of the challenge is to steer them away from an all-about text toward a step-by-step how-to text.

We recommend that you use coaching conferences to help youngsters become oriented to the writing you hope they do. When doing coaching conferences, you always want to try to keep your own prompts brief. You will probably need to get the child talking by asking a question or two, but your aim will be to set the child up to talk at some length so that you can pull back. You might simply say, "So how did you do it? Step 1 . . . ," and give the child an expectant look to keep him or her going.

When the child falters and has nothing to say, instead of asking another question, try just using gestures to signal, "More." or "Next?" It's tempting to ask question after question, but in life, one of the hard parts of writing is that there is not another person there, continually throwing the conversational ball back at the speaker.

As you do this, remember the importance of wait time. Many of us (grown-ups and teachers) have a tendency to want to fill up any moment of silence with more (grown-up) talk. Give children some time and space to think, and figure it out on their own. Aim to have your conferences comprised of 80% kid-talk and only 20% teacher-talk. Try this simple trick the next time you confer: count five full seconds of silence before you say anything. *Butterfly-one, butterfly-two, butterfly-three, butterfly-four, butterfly-five.* You will be amazed at how often children have something to say before you reach *butterfly-five.* You would have missed what the child had to say if you had spoken any sooner.

Lastly, if you do coach the child to do some work, try to give the child a chance to do that work again without your coaching. So if you had to say, "Step 1," and then "Step 2," and "Step 3," once you have pulled the steps out of the child in that fashion, try saying, "So can you tell me the whole thing, without me asking you for each step? Start at the beginning."

Perhaps you might even leave an index card with a reminder of your prompts so that they can remember to use them on their own. And afterward, name the work that the child has just done, and explicitly link it to the ongoing work of the unit. You might say, "From now on, whenever you are writing a how-to book, one thing you can try is. . . ."

MID-WORKSHOP TEACHING   Getting Ideas for How-To Books

"Writers, can I stop all of you for a moment?" I waited until all the children had set down their pens. "Chloe just had a really great idea. Did you know that we can also write how-to books about the things we've learned how to do in books? Chloe was looking at *The Pumpkin Book* by Gail Gibbons (2000). Thumbs up if you remember that book." Almost every thumb went up. "Remember how this book teaches us how to carve a pumpkin?" I flipped the book open to that page to remind them. "Well, that means that we all know how to carve a pumpkin now! Because we learned it from a book! As you are writing today, you could look at the books in our museum and think to yourself, 'Did I learn how to do anything from reading these books?' That's another great way to get ideas. You can write about things you know how to do from *life*, and you can write about things you know how to do from *books*."

Thinking about Potential How-To Books Across the Day

Recruit writers to come up with new topics for how-to books.

"Writers are always on the lookout for things to write about, and how-to book writers are always on the lookout for things they can *teach* about, right? Because how-to books always teach readers to do something new. Just looking around the room today at all of the things in our museum helped spark so many ideas for things you could teach readers about by writing how-to books. And you can think that way *all day long*! Maybe at lunch when you're looking in your lunchbox you'll remember that you could teach someone how to pack a lunch. You could write a how-to book about that! Or when you're waiting for the bus, you might realize that you could write a how-to book about that, too! Writers always keep their eyes open. You know what else? Writers are not just thinking about what they can teach. They are also thinking about what *readers need*. I was thinking last night about my nephew. He just got his very own library card. I was thinking I could write a how-to book for him about how to check out a library book, since he's just learning about that. Right now, why don't you think of someone in your life that could be a reader of your how-to books. What could you teach that reader about? Turn and talk to your partner."

After the students talked for a minute, I reconvened the class and called on a couple of students to share.

"I'm going to write a book for my cousin about how to use the potty! She wears pull-ups now," offered Rebecca.

"I can make a book for my baby brother about how to crawl!" called out William.

"Writers, what fantastic ideas you have. You are really thinking about your readers and what they need. I'm sure they'll find your new books super helpful."

Step 1   First roll a ball of snow.

Step 2   Now keep rolling it.

Step 3   And stop. Next …

Step 4   Start rolling another one.

Step 5   And keep rolling it.

Step 6   Next stack it.

Step 7   Next put the rocks on.

Step 8   Next put the carrot.

Step 9   Next put the hat.

FIG. 13–2   The books and objects at the classroom museum can inspire new ideas for how-to books. A book about snow could inspire "How to Make a Snowman." A book about pumpkins might lead to "How to Make a Jack-o-Lantern."

Writing a Series or Collection of How-To Books to Teach Others Even More about a Topic

IN THIS SESSION, you'll teach students that writers sometimes collect a series of books focused on one umbrella topic in order to teach others even more about their topic.

GETTING READY

✔ Gather several how-to texts on a single topic. These could be books written by yourself, your students, or even a trade book series such as the Pebble Plus series for science. Alyssa Capucilli's *My First Soccer Game* and *My First Ballet Class* (2011) books work well too. You might even decide to ask students to help you gather how-to texts on an easy-to-find topic (such as plants or cooking) during library time, technology time, reading workshop, or at home and bring them in for today's session. If you do this, you'll want to recruit kids the day before, of course (see Connection).

✔ Student writer that you have identified from the previous session who has written two or three how-to texts on a single topic (see Teaching)

✔ Children's writing folders (see Active Engagement)

✔ A student's collection of same-topic how-to titles that includes a title that doesn't fit (see Share)

COMMON CORE STATE STANDARDS: W.K.2, RI.K.1, RI.K.2, SL.K.1, SL.K.2, L.K.1, L.K.2, L.K.6

I N THE PREVIOUS SESSION the possibilities for what children could teach others was cracked wide open. And chances are that some of your children discovered that they have a dissertation's worth of information to teach on particular topics. When we give children an explicit invitation to consider their lives in school and out, and to consider the needs of their readers, experts are bound to emerge!

And experts, of course, have so much to say that they can't possibly be limited to one how-to book about their topics of expertise. When we encourage students to write multiple how-to books about the same topic, we are encouraging them to examine a topic from a variety of angles. Until now, you have nudged kids to write about many different topics. This lesson gives children permission to do what so many of them love to do already—write "another one" about the same topic again and again.

The process of taking on one topic in several ways actually inspires high-level thinking. Sophisticated writers keep returning to moments from their lives. Carl Anderson (*Strategic Writing Conferences,* 2009) encourages kids to embrace their "writing territories," writing as much as possible about the topics, places, people, and memories that matter most to them. There is complex thinking involved in say, choosing a topic (e.g., sports), and then writing how-to books related to different subcategories (soccer, baseball). Even kindergartners can think strategically about the main ideas of the books they write as related to an overarching topic, which is one of the main goals of a rich writing curriculum. According to Norman Webb (*Depth of Knowledge Web Alignment Tool,* 2005), strategic thinking requires "reasoning, developing a plan or sequence of steps to approach problems; requires some decision making and justification; abstract, complex, or non-routine; often more than one possible answer," which is exactly what children do when they create a series of how-to books on a topic.

In this session you'll teach children that there is no need to limit themselves to one how-to book per topic, that sometimes writers write a whole collection of how-to books all related to one topic. Recipe books, science experiment books, craft books, and even the class mentor text, *My First Soccer Game,* are all a part of a series. Writers love to write multiple how-to books to make a series or a chapter book. Today you'll show your students they can do this too.

Writing a Series or Collection of How-To Books to Teach Others Even More about a Topic

CONNECTION

Show students a selection of how-to books about the same topic, asking them what they notice.

"Writers. I'm going to show you three different books. I want you to see if you notice anything that is the same about them." Reading the titles aloud, I lined up three books along the chalkboard: *How to Make Slime* (2010), *How to Make Bubbles* (2011), and *How to Make a Liquid Rainbow* (2011). "Do you guys notice anything that is the same? Turn and tell your partner what you notice that is the same about all three of these." After a few moments I reconvened the class. "So, are they all how-to books? Yes! Are they all how-to books for science? Yes! Wow! This author must really love science. She wrote three different how-to books about different science experiments!

"You know, this gives me an idea. Some of you really love certain things. Some of you really want to write lots of how-to books about one thing. What if *you* wanted to write how-to books in a series like this? Could you do that too? Yes, you could!"

❧ **Name the teaching point.**

"Today I'm going to teach you that when you really love a topic, when it is something that is a big part of your life, or if it something that you really know a lot about, you can write lots of how-to books about it by thinking of that topic in many different ways."

TEACHING

Share an example of writing from one student who has already written multiple how-to books about a single topic. Recruit the class to help generate next steps.

"So, writers, look at what Rachel has already done. Rachel and I were looking at her folder yesterday, and we noticed that she already had three how-to books about cooking! She wrote three how-to books to teach us how to make different kinds of food. She has one piece titled 'How to Make an Ice Cream.' Remember when she read that to us a few days ago? Well, now she has another one titled, 'How to Make a Cupcake.' She even has a third, titled 'How to Make a Smoothie.'"

◆ COACHING

You might, of course, select books on another topic—one that especially appeals to your particular class of students—whose common theme your kids will readily identify.

FIG. 14–1 Rachel writes a series of books on cooking: "How to Make an Ice Cream."

"Rachel and I already talked, and she decided that she wants to make even more how-to books about cooking. But here is the only problem. Even though Rachel loves cooking, she is having trouble thinking of more how-to books she could make. Do you think you guys could help her? What do you do when you are stuck for ideas? Where could we look for ideas? What could we do? Turn and tell your partner your ideas for Rachel's next how-to book about cooking."

As kids turned and talked with each other, I listened in to gather ideas from what they were saying and coached Rachel to join me in listening to her classmates. I voiced over, as they were talking, "Remember, you can think of things you know from school—even from school lunch and school breakfast!" Before long, I whispered to Rachel, "Which one do you think you'll write next? Do you think you'll do 'How to Make a Salad from the Salad Bar,' like Damien said or 'How to Put Milk in Your Cereal,' like Cooper said?" Rachel thought for a moment, then said, decisively, "Salad bar."

Share one child's next steps, and quickly demonstrate how to get started making a collection of how-to books.

"Wow! You guys are really coming up with a lot of ideas for more how-to books! Rachel and I were listening to get ideas, and now she's going to write *another* cooking how-to book! She's going to write 'How to Make a Salad from the Salad Bar!'" I held up a blank booklet and pointed to where Rachel's new title would go. "In Rachel's new book she'll write all the steps for making a salad at the school lunch salad bar. When she's finished, she'll have a whole collection of cooking how-to books! She might even think of more!

"So, writers, today we learned that writers often don't just write one how-to book about topics that they really love. Did you see how Rachel realized that she already had a few how-to books about something, so she pushed herself to come up with an idea for another how-to book for her collection? Lots of writers write this way. In fact, some of you might even have a collection started already!"

ACTIVE ENGAGEMENT

Ask students to plan for writing another how-to book on a topic they've already written a book about.

"Writers, right now, look through your writing folder to see if you could make another how-to book to fit with one of the how-to books you already wrote, so that you could have a series of how-to books too, just like Rachel. When you find one, take it out and put it on top of your writing folder like this." As children searched, I moved around the meeting area. A few children immediately pulled out their favorite how-to book, confident that they had more how-to books to add to that one. As more and more children found how-to books to pull out and closed their folders, I called for everyone's attention. "Now that you've picked out one how-to book, what will your next how-to book be? When you have a good title for your next how-to book, give me a thumbs up."

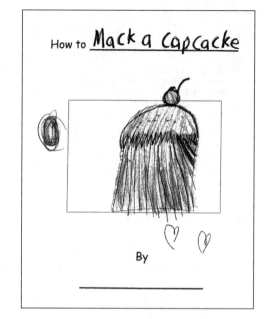

FIG. 14–2 "How to Make a Cupcake"

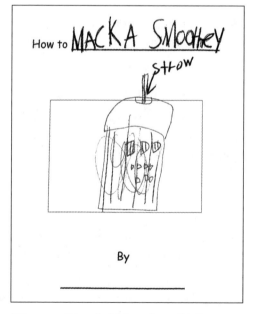

FIG. 14–3 "How to Make a Smoothie"

Restate the process of creating a collection of how-to books explicitly, step by step, to make it more transferable.

"So first, we looked through our folders to see if there was a how-to book we really loved. Then we took it out, and we thought of another how-to book we could make. When we finish that one, we can see if there's another one and another one. Pretty soon, you'll have a whole series of how-to books just like the science experiment series or Rachel's series about cooking!"

LINK

Rally children to try writing multiple how-to books about one topic, using the many resources available to them.

"Writers, today many of you will write a second and even a third how-to book on something that you really love. Maybe you'll write three different how-to books for football, like 'How to Throw a Football,' 'How to Tackle,' and 'How to Put on Your Football Equipment.' Or maybe you'll do three different how-to books about your pet, like 'How to Feed a Dog,' 'How to Play with a Dog,' and 'How to Wash a Dog.' Maybe some of you will pick your favorite things we've been studying in school, like community jobs in social studies, and you'll do 'How to Mail a Letter,' and 'How to Get a Library Card.' I bet you're already thinking of all the different possibilities!

"As always, writers, remember that you know many strategies for doing the best work that you can do. Don't forget that we have many charts hanging around the room for you to refer to so you can remember to use all the strategies you know!"

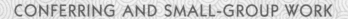

Helping Students Stay Independently Focused on Writing Work

W E EXPECT SO MUCH OF OUR YOUNGEST WRITERS, but the fact that they are up to the task doesn't mean that we won't need to be there to nudge, remind, corral, and guide them into independence throughout the year. The groundwork we lay at the beginning of the year, as far as classroom and workshop expectations go, is crucial to building a functional writing community that promotes independence. But as the year progresses kids will find new ways to get off task, and we'll need to find new ways to refocus them. From a few steps away, Destiny and Roberto seemed to be in the midst of a deeply engaged partner discussion of Destiny's how-to book. Heads bent over the paper, Roberto even appeared to be pointing things out that Destiny had tried.

As I listened in for a moment, though, I heard Roberto say, "And then the spider comes down and hops on this line, and then it climbs up the side of this guy here." "Yeah! And then he goes under the table!" added Destiny, pointing below the picture of a table she had drawn to show how to set the table for dinner time.

Though I already knew what I'd be addressing first, I knelt down by the children and said, "Destiny and Roberto, it looks like you two are giving each other some ideas. That's great! What are you working on?" "Well, we just saw a spider," Destiny started. "And he walked away over there, but we can't find him," finished Roberto.

"Ohhhh. So there's not a real spider in Destiny's how-to book?" I asked, pretending to be confused. "Well, no, but he was on my desk!" Destiny said.

"Writers," I said. "It looks like you got a little distracted by something that happened as you were writing. That happens to all writers! It's hard work to stay focused when something interesting happens—like having a spider walk over your paper! But when writers get distracted like that, they don't have to wait for a grown-up to remind them to stay focused on writing. They kind of have to be their own grown-up and say, 'Oops. I better get back to my writing. There are so many things I could be working on!' And you know what? Writing partners can help each other that way, too. You can always remind each other about what is the most important thing to be paying attention to during writing time: writing! You can keep working together, of course, but make sure you're talking about writing."

If it was earlier in the year, I might have extended the conference and gotten into another teaching point, but by this time I knew that these students would be able to get started on their own, so I chose to move on.

MID-WORKSHOP TEACHING **Turning a Series of How-To Books into One Big How-To Chapter Book**

"Writers, I just have to show you this. I was working with this group over here, and we came up with this really cool idea that I think you might want to try. We made chapter books out of our how-to books! Sam had three separate how-to books. He had 'How to Draw a Bear,' 'How to Draw a Car,' and 'How to Draw a Star.' All books about how to draw. So he took a blank sheet of paper for a cover, and he stacked up all three how-to books, and he stapled them all together! He wrote the title on the cover to fit with all the how-to books inside: 'Drawing.' What do you think about that? Look, Melissa did it too! She did 'Taking Care of a Dog.' And Jeremy did 'School'! Who else might want to make a how-to chapter book? Awesome! I'll put some staplers and some blank paper for covers, so that if you want to do it, all you have to do is go to the writing center."

As Students Continue Working . . .

"Writers, some of you wanted to make a how-to chapter book, but you only have one how-to book to go with it. That's okay. Right now, you can make another how-to book to fit with it! You can just keep on adding on as many how-to books as you can to your chapter book, as long as they all fit with your title."

Making Sure All Books in a Collection Go Together

Read (or have a student read) titles in a collection of how-to books in which one doesn't fit, and then ask students to notice and discuss why.

Before students gathered in the meeting area I'd made sure to check in with Jennifer, who I had conferred with, to ask if she would share her work.

"Writers," I said, "Jennifer is up here with me right now because she figured something out when she was working on a how-to chapter book today. Jennifer was rereading the how-to books that she'd stapled together into one big chapter book of how-to books all about things to do in the park. She discovered something! Jennifer, will you just read the titles of your how-to books to us?"

She read, "'How to Ride a Scooter,' 'How to Do Monkey Bars,' 'How to Make a Picnic,'" and then, giggling a little, "'How to Read Your Sister a Bedtime Story.'"

"What did you notice as Jennifer was rereading?"

Hands flew up. One student said, "You don't read bedtime stories in the *park*!"

"Is that what you noticed, too, Jennifer?" I asked. She nodded.

"So what are you planning to do?"

"I'm going to take out this one because it doesn't fit."

"Such a great idea. Writers, you can all do what Jennifer did. If you are making a chapter book of how-to books that are all about the same thing, you can reread and make sure all of the chapters actually go with the big topic. And if you find one that doesn't fit, you can take it right out! Thanks for helping us figure that out, Jennifer."

Writers Can Write Introductions and Conclusions to Help Their Readers

IN THIS SESSION, you'll teach students that writers clarify a topic new to readers by writing introductions and conclusions.

GETTING READY

✔ One student-made how-to book about a topic that will require background information to understand (e.g., "How to Play Angry Birds") (see Connection)

✔ Class text, "How to Make a Peanut Butter and Jelly Sandwich" as well as blank pages to add on (see Teaching and Active Engagement)

✔ Students' writing folders (see Share)

✔ One child's exemplary ending (see Share)

COMMON CORE STATE STANDARDS: W.K.2, W.K.5, W.1.2, RI.K.1, SL.K.1, L.K.1, L.K.2, L.K.6

F OR THE PAST TWO SESSIONS, you've emphasized the idea that writers of how-to books give their readers new information. You've helped children see themselves as experts on familiar topics, as well as brand-new things they've recently learned in school. And in the last session, you helped your students learn to linger on a topic, creating many how-to books and maybe even stapling them together to create a chapter book. Think of it—chapter books! How very grown-up your kindergartners are becoming!

When you sit down to talk with your kindergartners about their interests—things about which they have a lot of information to share—it is inevitable that you'll encounter pop culture references that you haven't a clue about. From Pokémon cards and SpongeBob SquarePants, to Angry Birds. The list goes on, and as fads come and fads go, so too will the topics that your children are dying to write about. Now it is probably time to let your kindergartners in on something that is bound to surprise them. You'll gather them close and break the news to them. "Kids," you might say. "This might surprise you, but I have to tell you. Some of your topics are new to a lot of people. Not everybody knows how to play Angry Birds. In fact, some people might not even know what Angry Birds *is*! Can you believe that?"

In this session you'll invite a child to play the role of the reader of the class how-to book, and together, you and your class will write an introduction that helps that reader understand the topic better. This teaching move, among others in this lesson, is one that will carry into other lessons. Inviting kids to act out the roles of reader and writer helps make the concept of audience more concrete. We so often refer to readers assuming that kids will know what we mean when we say things like, "Make things easier for the reader to understand," or "easier for the reader to read," or to "teach the reader more information." Have a child pretend to be the actual reader, or do it yourself, so kids can see the reader at work, trying to understand, with their very own eyes.

You will notice that this session teaches more than one strategy for writing an introduction. The teaching part of this minilesson introduces one strategy: writing an introduction that teaches the reader information. The active engagement builds on that initial teaching point by adding in that writers also try to make an introduction interesting by putting in where the idea came from or why the topic is important.

"Inviting kids to act out the roles of reader and writer helps make the concept of audience more concrete."

This work stands on the shoulders of the Common Core State Standards for informational writing for kindergarten and first grade. We find it helpful to think long term about children's writing. Take a look ahead to first- and second-grade standards, and you'll see that there is plenty of work that kindergartners could get started on right away, rather than waiting to tackle. When we introduce some of the work that lies ahead early on, we open up the opportunity for children to give things a try, to approximate. Though their attempts will be less than perfect, the early start will give kids multiple chances to revisit the work across this year and the next, each time around becoming more independent. If you teach children to write introductions for their how-to books now, they will easily be able to meet the Common Core State Standards (which include writing an introduction) for informational writing by the end of first grade.

For now, you'll teach children to write very simple introductions that invite the reader to learn about the topic and perhaps give some necessary facts or a definition. There will be plenty of time in the months and years ahead for children to learn the specific ways authors introduce and conclude a text. For today, the most important thing will be for your kindergartners to grasp that they are expected to include an introduction or a beginning of some sort in their how-to text. We suggest splitting up your teaching of introductions and conclusions, teaching one in the minilesson and perhaps adding on the other as a mid-workshop teaching point or a share. Today will be a big step for your young writers: to realize that they know about topics that others have never heard of, that they truly are teachers to the people who read their work. Enjoy teaching this lesson, and let your children's approximations be fuel for ideas for future lessons and conferring.

Writers Can Write Introductions and Conclusions to Help Their Readers

CONNECTION

Show students that introductions are necessary by explaining that you, along with many other grown-ups, have *never even heard of* a familiar fad that is currently popular with your class.

"Writers, this morning, Preston couldn't wait for me to read his 'How to Play Angry Birds' book. He ran up to me, saying, 'Look! I wrote a book at home!' Then he read it, and this is how it went. 'First stretch the bird back. Then you let the bird go. Then you see the bird go when it is crossing.'"

I stopped and gave the kids a look of exaggerated confusion. "What? I do not understand! You have to stretch a bird? What are you talking about?" I smiled, knowing it would sound funny to the class, and kids laughed.

"Writers, you won't believe this, but before reading Preston's book, I had never even heard of Angry Birds." I paused for dramatic effect, and the children let out a collective gasp of incredulity. "Preston had to explain to me that Angry Birds is a game that you play on a phone or a computer, and the birds are just pretend. You use a pretend slingshot to toss the birds and knock down bricks so that the pigs hiding under the bricks will pop. The goal of the game is to pop all the pigs. Phew. After he explained what the game was, everything else made perfect sense!

"So Preston wrote a little introduction for people like me, who don't know about Angry Birds. It goes like this. 'Angry Birds is a super game to play. You play it on the computer or an iPad.'"

If you and your class have never heard of Angry Birds, choose a different example to use for this lesson. The topic is less important—it is the teaching that matters.

> Angry Birds is a super game to play. You play it on the computer or an iPad.
>
> First stretch the bird back.
>
> Next you let the bird go.
>
> Then you see the bird go when it is crossing.

♣ **Name the teaching point.**

"Today I want to teach you that writers of how-to books often write a special page to introduce their books to help their readers understand their topic—just like Preston helped me understand his book. How-to writers often pretend that the people who will read the book have never even heard of the topic, and then they write an introduction page to give the readers some information or facts so that the rest of the how-to book will make more sense."

TEACHING

Invite a student to role-play being an uninformed reader, and recruit the class to help generate an introduction that provides background knowledge.

"Class, will you help me to write an introduction for our 'How to Make a Peanut Butter and Jelly Sandwich' book? First, we need a reader. Preston? Will you be our reader?" Preston agreed and came to the front of the meeting area to sit next to me.

"Okay, Preston. Pretend that you have never even heard of a peanut butter and jelly sandwich before. Are you ready?" Preston nodded. I read aloud just the first few pages of our class how-to book.

How to Make a Peanut Butter and Jelly Sandwich

1. Get the jar of peanut butter. Be careful you don't drop the jar!

2. Open it, and using your knife, scoop out a knife-full of peanut butter. Be sure the knife is clean.

3. Spread the peanut butter over one piece of bread.

Stopping here, I said, "Preston, if you didn't even know what a PB&J was, would that make sense? Would you know what to do?" Preston shook his head, no. I turned to the rest of the class, "What do you think?"

Model writing a very simple introduction, leaving out crucial information.

Holding up a fresh sheet of paper, I said to the class, "I think we better add a page to our book that tells our reader, Preston, what a PB&J actually is. That way, before he reads the steps, he'll know what he's making. Hmm." I paused, thinking. "Got it. I could write, 'This book will teach you how to make a peanut butter and jelly sandwich.'" I gestured across the page to show that I was planning to write this. "Preston, now do you know what a peanut butter and jelly sandwich is? Are you ready for the steps?" Preston shook his head. "Nooo! You still didn't tell me."

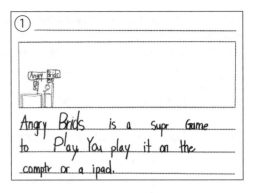

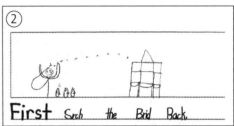

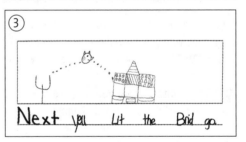

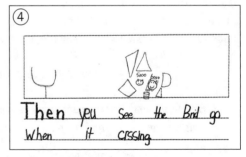

FIG. 15–1 Preston writes an introduction for his book on angry birds.

"Oh, okay. No problem. Let me try again. A peanut butter and jelly sandwich is a delicious and easy to make sandwich made with bread, peanut butter, and jelly." I looked at the class and Preston. "Is that better?" The class agreed, and I quickly wrote our introduction across the page and added it to the class how-to book.

ACTIVE ENGAGEMENT

Recruit children to help write an even better introduction for the class book.

"Writers, this introduction is pretty good, but I think it could be even better. When Preston told me about his how-to book this morning, he was so excited about it. He really made me want to read it! Maybe we could try writing our introduction so that it really makes people want to read it, too.

"I'm going to let you in on a secret. Writers have a few tricks for getting people to really want to read their books. They might tell people where their idea came from or why it is important information for people to know. Will you turn and tell your partner what you think we could say to make our introduction even better? What could we say to get readers to really want to read our book?"

After children discuss, elicit a few responses.

I motioned to Nicole to start. "It's important to know how to make peanut butter and jelly so you can eat it for lunch." "Yes, that introduction will certainly make somebody who is looking for ideas for lunch want to read our book, Nicole," I said. "And it certainly lets everyone know why this how-to book is important."

"It's important to know how to make peanut butter and jelly so you can eat it when you don't like anything else," Damien added. "Yes. That will definitely make people want to read our book," I acknowledged.

"Yummy, yummy. Do you want to make something yummy?" Cooper called out, breaking the pattern. We all laughed a little. "Yes, Cooper! That makes the book sound really interesting and fun to read, doesn't it? Let's add that to our introduction!" I quickly added a sentence to the introduction page. The book now read:

How to Make a Peanut Butter and Jelly Sandwich

Yummy, yummy. Do you want to make something yummy? A peanut butter and jelly sandwich is a delicious and easy to make sandwich made with bread, peanut butter, and jelly.

1. Get the jar of peanut butter. Be sure that you don't drop the jar.

2. Open it, and using your knife, scoop out a knife-full of peanut butter. Be sure the knife is clean.

3. Spread the peanut butter over one piece of bread

4. Open the jelly jar and use your knife to scoop out some jelly.

In this session, we use the active engagement to build on the initial teaching point, lifting the work that we shared in the first part of the mini-lesson. This makes it possible to teach a whole repertoire of strategies in one lesson rolling out little tips one at a time.

You will want to spend some time during interactive writing adding the last steps to this book. Not all writing needs to happen during writing workshop.

5. Spread the jelly over the other piece of bread.

6. Squish the two pieces of bread together. Make sure the peanut butter and jelly are on the inside!

Debrief in ways that emphasize the parts of this work that can transfer to other books, on other days.

"Writers, you've all found a way to write a sentence or two that could go at the start of our how-to book as an introduction. You can let readers know where your idea came from, or why the book is important to read, or even tell your readers a bit of information, so that they won't get confused like I was when I first read Preston's Angry Bird book."

LINK

Rally writers to move beyond the topic of today's lesson, suggesting several possible ways that writers could spend their time today.

"Writers, today you should be doing everything that how-to writers do. For a few minutes, perhaps early on, you might try writing an introduction, but that will take a few minutes, not a whole day. So why don't I list the sort of work you might do after that, and if I say something that *you* were thinking you would do after you write a quick introduction, get up and get started."

"Some of you are probably going to reread the book you were writing yesterday and then keep going in it. If so, get busy." A few kids skipped off.

"Some of you will be figuring out what your next how-to book will be about. You might decide to look through the museum of objects and books at your tables, just to get some ideas. If a book says, 'How to Make Jello,' that book might give you the idea for writing about making brownies or French toast. If you will be starting new books, off you go." Another contingent left the meeting area.

"And some of you might decide that you want to write introductions for *all* of your old how-to books before you start another how-to book, so that your readers won't be confused, like I was when Preston read me his Angry Birds book. Remember, there might be people who have never even heard of your topic! The rest of you, what will you be doing?"

By listing off options for writing time and asking students to choose what they will be doing today before they leave the meeting area, we hope to guard against students getting to their writing spots and just sitting there, not sure what their plan for the day will be. This type of transition also allows students who are unsure of what they need to do to remain in the meeting are after others disperse, to receive additional support.

Teaching the Writer, Not the Writing

THE IMPORTANT THING TO REMEMBER ABOUT TODAY'S LESSON—and this entire bend—is that your children are writing to *teach* people. There will be many children who understand this well and invent ways to grab readers' attention and fill their how-to books to the brim with information and details. There will also be pockets of children who are working hard on their books but struggle with the concept that someone will indeed read their book and that this someone may or may not be familiar with the topic of the book. You'll be tempted to linger with these students, trying again and again to get them to write introductions that provide a definition or some facts, only to wind up with introductions that restate the title: "This book is about Nintendo." Or "This book is about Nintendo. A Nintendo is like DS or like a Wii." Try as you might, some of your kindergarteners might not produce the informative introductions that you imagined.

Fear not, for this is a difficult concept, even for adult writers and readers. Sometimes the topics that are the most familiar are the hardest to write about with clarity because it is so difficult to imagine *not* knowing. My advice is to be sure that you are prioritizing the intentions of the writer, *not* the day's minilesson. Just as children benefit from revisiting things we've taught long ago, so too is it helpful to remind ourselves of things we've learned in other contexts. Remembering to teach the writer, not the writing, is crucial. While we may be tempted to spend lots of energy guiding children to do whatever we've just taught, we need to remind ourselves to put the child's intentions and individual learning trajectory ahead of anything else.

It is important as well to make explicit to the children you are conferring with that whatever you've just taught them in conferences or small groups is just one thing among many that they can be working on. As you wrap up your conferences or small groups and link to ongoing work, think about what you have taught and be explicit with your students about how to use their new learning in context. Are you setting the child up with a strategy or set of strategies to use in addition to all the minilessons you have taught? Or does what you have taught serve as an accommodation for the child—something to use *in place* of what you've been showing in minilessons—such as introducing a more highly scaffolded paper choice that the rest of the class is not using.

Keeping clear conferring notes is so important. Our teaching is much "stickier" and more powerful when we begin conferences by following up on earlier teaching. One research question you ask children might always be, "Last time we worked together I taught you . . . Can you show me a place where you're still doing that?"

If you plan to teach about writing conclusions within the share today, you'll want to confer into this idea with one child so that you have an example to show the class.

MID-WORKSHOP TEACHING **When Necessary, Writers Unstick Themselves by Skipping the Introduction**

"Writers, eyes on me." I waited. "A few of you are stuck over how to write an introduction. Here is a really important tip: writers figure out ways to unstick themselves. Can you think about how you could unstick yourself if you are doing nothing because you don't know what to write on page 1, on your introduction page? Think really hard. You are sitting with a blank book, stuck. You are thinking, 'Oh no, oh no, I do not know how to write my page 1. Oh no, oh no.' What can you do to unstick yourself?"

I called on Oliver, who was practically climbing out of his chair. "Skip it?" he said.

"Absolutely. Just skip it! If you can't think of your page 1, then skip it and move on to the rest of the book. You can always come back later, maybe with your partner helping, and decide what to say and then you can just slip an introduction page into the front of a finished how-to booklet. Some how-to books have introductions, and some don't. You can decide what to work on, all by yourself."

Writing Conclusions

Using the work of one child, explain that in addition to introductions that get readers ready to learn, how-to book writers can write conclusions that let readers know the book is over.

"Oh, my goodness, you have got to race over here to see what Vivian did today. Bring the book you are working on and a pen and come quickly." Once the children had arrived, I called Vivian forward and said, "Vivian was really thinking about her readers. She got to the end of her book about Beyblades, and she thought, 'Hey, I think I will write a little message to my reader at the end of my book. That way the reader will know that the book is over.' She decided that to have good manners as a writer she could say a thank-you or a good-bye at the end of her book. So she ended her book this way. Listen." (See Figure 15–2 on following page.)

Vivian, sitting up proudly, read, "Have fun playing!"

> Beyblades are a game with pieces that crash into each other.
>
> First you you need the ripper and take the Beyblade.
>
> Next if you want to have two player you can have two player.
>
> Then you pick up the thing.
>
> Then you say "Beyblade let it rip."
>
> Last you play with your friend.
>
> Have fun playing!

"Nice job, Vivian. Writers, let's all try Vivian's strategy, right now. Quick as a wink, take out a how-to book you feel is almost done, and write *your* last page." As children worked, I looked over their shoulders, sometimes reading their endings aloud to help other children get ideas.

1. Bey blad are a game that crash in to each other.

2. First you need the riper and take the beyblad.

3. Next if you want to have two player you can have two player.

4. Then your pick up the thing.

5. Then you say beyblad let it rip.

6. Last you play with your frind

7. Have fun playing!

FIG. 15–2   Vivian writes a conclusion for her book on Beyblades.

Writers Use Everything They Know to Make Their How-To Books Easy to Read

MANY TEACHERS regard interactive writing as an essential way to provide intensive literacy support and devote ten or fifteen minutes to an interactive writing session almost every day. This time is separate and in addition to the writing workshop. During interactive writing, a teacher might recruit several children to come and write on chart paper at the front of the room while the other children either write some of the text on white boards or pretend to write along with the teacher and helpers at the front of the room.

Today, we've provided an example of how an interactive writing session might serve in place of a minilesson from time to time.

At the start of the year, when interactive writing is first introduced, children learn to bring their white boards to the rug, along with thin dry erase markers. We also suggest pieces of felt (to use as erasers) hot-glued to the markers for convenient management. You will, of course, develop your own system, one that works best for you and your students. We also suggest that charts—including an alphabet chart—be attached to the backs of the boards, in plastic sleeves. As time goes on, other charts, such as personal word walls or consonant blends and digraph charts, can be slipped into the sleeves, along with the alphabet charts. Setting the tools up carefully saves distribution time and makes management easy. Children learn from the beginning not to touch the markers until it is time and not to use the markers for anything but interactive *writing* (e.g., no drawing on your neighbor's arm). The first few times children do interactive writing, they learn that to keep using the materials, they must use them appropriately.

Interactive writing is often called "sharing the pen" or "writing all together" because the teacher leads the whole class in deciding on a message to write on the easel, planning it by touching the page to say what will go there, then writing each word (conventionally) together. The children join in, writing particular sounds on their white boards—(and later, even whole words and phrases) along with the teacher. Usually, during an interactive writing session several children will be invited to the easel to write parts of the message. For

IN THIS SESSION, you'll teach students that writers are always working to make their writing easy to read, using all the strategies they know.

GETTING READY

✔ Large alphabet chart on display near the meeting area

✔ Word wall with familiar high-frequency words on display near the meeting area

✔ "Making Writing Easy to Read" chart from *Writing for Readers* unit (see Connection)

✔ Enlarged version of shared class text "How to Make a Peanut Butter and Jelly Sandwich" (see Teaching/Interactive Writing)

✔ "Learning from a Mentor How-To Text" chart (see Teaching/Interactive Writing)

✔ Small white boards for each child, dry erase markers, and felt erasers (see Teaching/Interactive Writing)

✔ "The Peanut Butter and Jelly Song" lyrics enlarged on chart paper (see Share). Of course, if this is not the text you have been using for your demonstration, then you could eliminate this part.

✔ Post-its (see Share)

COMMON CORE STATE STANDARDS: W.K.2; RFS.K.1; RFS.K.3; RFS.1.3; SL.K.1; L.K.1; L.K.2

efficiency's sake, many teachers like to choose two or three children to come to the easel at the beginning of the session, to be helpers for the entire message.

Often you will choose sentences strategically, making sure that the appropriate opportunities to practice letter sounds, spelling patterns, spacing, capitalization, and punctuation present themselves. For example, in the *Writing for Readers* unit, the children learned to listen for initial sounds in words. It makes sense then, in interactive writing, to include words that contain initial consonant sounds that children will have success identifying and writing.

"An interactive writing session might serve in place of a minilesson from time to time."

Interactive writing slows the writing process down, because children join in thinking through the letter sounds and other conventions. There's no need to write an entire book in one sitting with interactive writing. The class can return to an interactive writing project to write parts of it bit by bit. After texts are eventually finished, they become favorites for shared

reading, and you can make small copies for children to read on their own.

In this interactive writing session, the class how-to book has been worked on one page at a time, over the course of a few weeks. Some of this has taken place during regular minilessons, following the usual structure of a minilesson, while some of it was done during a separate interactive writing time. As is the case here, sometimes you will do nearly all the writing based on the children's suggestions, and other times children participate by writing the words on the chart paper with your support. Class texts are often worked on in various ways throughout the day. The same text might be used for an interactive writing session with the whole class, then again as a demonstration text in a minilesson, again as a demonstration piece for small-group work, and again and again throughout the day for various purposes.

Today's lesson does not follow the usual structure of a minilesson. There is still a connection, to remind students of some familiar content to connect to, and there is still a link at the end to connect the lesson to the ongoing work of the unit. But instead of the structure of teaching by demonstration followed by actively involving the students in trying the strategy, you'll lead the class in an interactive writing session that highlights their entire editing repertoire, all that they have learned about making their writing easy for others to read.

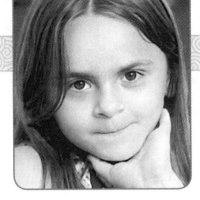

Writers Use Everything They Know to Make Their How-To Books Easy to Read

CONNECTION

Prepare students for interactive writing and draw their attention to the chart, "Making Writing Easy to Read"

I called the children over to the meeting area, saying, "Today bring your white boards to the rug, just like we do during interactive writing." When the class had gathered, I began. "Writers, today I want to remind you of all the strategies you learned earlier in the year for making your writing easier to read." I gestured to our "Making Writing Easy to Read" chart.

Throughout the school year you will be creating many process and anchor charts with your students. As units draw to a close, most of these charts will be packed away, only brought out on special occasions for review. However, a select few will remain visible and easy access for your students all year, as the content is not genre- or unit-specific. This chart is one such example.

> ### Make Writing Easy to Read
>
> Hear lots of sounds in a word
>
> Leave spaces between words
>
> Make pictures that hold the words of the story
>
> Use capitals at the start of a sentence
>
> **Flip between writing and reading, writing and reading**

"Remember we also learned to use personal word walls, too?"

❖ Name the teaching point.

"Today I want to teach you that writers don't just wait until they are finished to go back and make their writing easy to read. They work on it all the time, using all their strategies combined."

TEACHING/INTERACTIVE WRITING

"Today I'd like you to share the pen with me as we add on to our class book, 'How to Make a Peanut Butter and Jelly Sandwich.' As we write the last few steps of our how-to book, I need you help me to make it as easy to read as possible. Jarett and Melanie, come on up. You are going to be my interactive writing helpers today."

Jarett and Melanie stood to the side of the easel, waiting. We had had regular interactive writing sessions nearly every morning, so they knew the routine.

"Writers, let's reread 'How to Make a Peanut Butter and Jelly Sandwich' together, thinking, 'Hmm, what more could we add?' Jarett, you can use the pointer. Remember to point under each word, one at a time, so that we can use one voice together as a class to reread our work."

Jarett pointed, and the whole class read along. I made an effort to keep my voice extra low so that I could hear children reading.

How to Make a Peanut Butter and Jelly Sandwich

Yummy, yummy. Do you want to make something yummy? A peanut butter and jelly sandwich is a delicious and easy to make sandwich made with bread, peanut butter, and jelly.

1. Get the jar of peanut butter. Be sure that you don't drop the jar.

2. Open it, and using your knife, scoop out a knife-full of peanut butter. Be sure the knife is clean.

3. Spread the peanut butter over one piece of bread.

4. Open the jelly jar and use your knife to scoop out some jelly.

5. Spread the jelly over the other piece of bread.

6. Squish the two pieces of bread together. Make sure the peanut butter and jelly are on the inside!

"Great. Now, what else could we write? Turn and talk to the person next to you. Remember to look at our 'Learning from a Mentor How-To Text' chart for ideas." I listened in, just for a moment. I had actually already pretty much planned what we were going to write, keeping in mind both time and the types of words that I knew I would want to practice with the class. Having children turn and talk was my way of getting them engaged and making sure that the text felt like it was created by the kids and not by the teacher alone. Then I said, "Eyes on me! Great. I heard someone say that we could write a conclusion! Great idea. Let's write, 'Now you can make a peanut butter and jelly sandwich.' Let's get ready to write those words." I pointed to the spots where the words would be written and said the sentence twice, encouraging the class to say them along with me. "Now, everybody, help Melanie and me write the conclusion for our book."

On this day I designed the sentence to lend itself to the repertoire of editing strategies the children already knew from previous units: using word wall words, initial and ending sounds, spaces, uppercase letters, and one newer thing—end punctuation. I usually write down the sentence I'm going to use and decide which parts I'll invite the kids to write interactively and which parts I will simply write. My plan looks like this, with the underlined parts fitting the goals of my lesson. These are the parts the children will write on their white boards, using their alphabet charts or word walls as tools: <u>Now</u> <u>you</u> <u>can</u> <u>make</u> a <u>peanut</u> <u>butter</u> and <u>jelly</u> sandwich.

How To Make A
Peanut Butter And Jelly
Sandwich

by Our Class

Introduction

Do you want to make something yummy?

Yummy, yummy. Do you want to make something yummy? A peanut butter and jelly sandwich is a delicious and easy to make sandwich made with bread, peanut butter, and jelly.

1

Peanut Butter

Get the jar of peanut butter. Be careful that you don't drop the jar.

2

Peanut Butter

Open it, and using your knife, scoop out a knife-full of peanut butter. Be sure that the knife is clean.

3

Spread the peanut butter over one piece of bread.

4

Jelly
Jelly

Open the jelly jar and use your knife to scoop out some jelly.

5

Spread the jelly over the other piece of bread.

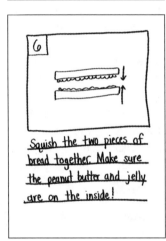

6

Squish the two pieces of bread together. Make sure the peanut butter and jelly are on the inside!

Conclusion

Hooray!

Now you can make a peanut butter and jelly sandwich.

FIG. 16–1   The class shared text continues to grow. Notice the combination of teacher and student handwriting where interactive writing was used.

Keep the entire class engaged by inviting them to write the sentence on their white boards.

"Let's say the first word and listen for the first sound. When you hear the first sound, write it on your white board, and Melanie will write it up here in our class how-to book. /N/ow." I said this slowly, and the children joined in, uncapping their markers and writing on their white boards. "Great job remembering that when we start a new sentence we use a capital letter, Melanie! Everybody, check your boards. Did you do it too? Is your *N* lowercase or uppercase? Switch it to uppercase if you need to, because we're starting a new sentence." I paused, and when all the caps were back on the markers, I wrote the rest of the word *Now* and continued.

"Erase your boards, everybody, to get ready to work on the next word. The next word is *you.* Hey! That's a word wall word. Everybody, point to it on the word wall now! Jarrett, look at the word wall, find the word *you,* and then write it in our book without looking back." While Jarett worked, I said to the rest of the class, "Write the word *you* on your white board now." I turned my attention back to Jarrett, who was just finishing. "Did you remember to check it on the word wall one last time, now that you've written it? Great. Nice work leaving a space between *Now* and *you*. That makes it easy to read. Marker caps on, everybody. Erase and get ready for the next word."

We moved on to *can* (another word wall word) much the same way, with Melanie taking a turn writing on the chart paper and the rest of the class writing the word on their white boards and checking it against the word wall. "Let's reread what we've written so far, shall we? Remember, it's important to flip between reading and writing, writing and reading," I said, pointing to the "Making Writing Easy to Read" chart. Jarret pointed, leading class in reading the text so far. They knew the next word would be *make*.

As we continued on, I recruited the children to join in hearing and recording initial sounds while I filled in the rest of the words—the parts that weren't part of my teaching focus for today. When Jarrett had trouble with the /j/ sound in *jelly*, Melanie suggested that he look at the alphabet chart to find a letter with a sound like *jelly*. When Melanie forgot to leave a space between *jelly* and *sandwich*, I left it that way, knowing that we could edit it upon rereading.

When we reached the end of the first sentence, I prompted the class to reread once more, with Jarett pointing again. When we got to "jellysandwich," Jarrett ran out of words to point to, and the class realized that something must be wrong. I pretended to look puzzled and said, "Hmm, sometimes this happens. I'm rereading my writing, and *Bam!* No more words! It could only be two things. Either I did not point carefully enough, or I forgot to leave a space between two words. Writers, right now, will you reread our sentence to see if you can figure out what went wrong?" They easily determined that there was a space missing. I coached Jarrett to draw a line to divide the two smooshed-together words, and we continued on, rereading one last time. This time, of course, the kids knew that our sentence was finished. We had used nearly everything on our checklist.

"What goes at the end of the sentence, when a thought is complete?" I wondered aloud. "A period!" the kids chimed in.

LINK

Reread the new sentence and encourage students to always use what they know to make their writing easy to read.

After we were done writing and rereading the final page of "How to Make a Peanut Butter and Jelly Sandwich" we reread our work one last time, "With feeling!" just to be sure we didn't miss anything. "Today and every day, and hopefully for the rest of your lives," I said to the class, "you will remember that you can write this way all the time. You can use everything you know to make your writing easy for others to read."

Using the Information Writing Rubric (and/or Benchmark Samples) to Guide Conferring and Small-Group Work

IN MANY SCHOOLS, teachers use a rubric containing a continuum of student work to help them determine how children are progressing in relationship to the end-of-year benchmark for each grade. Together, teachers ask, "What level of writing do we expect in September, January, and June of kindergarten?" Then pieces of writing that reflect their agreed upon expectations are chosen and used as tools for conferring and designing small-group work. It is also helpful to know the expectations for the grade above the one you teach. Some of your children may be approaching the September or even January benchmark for first grade.

As you study children's work in this unit, hold your expectations for June in mind. Perhaps you will carry an end of the year sample around with you as you confer and use this in two ways: (1) use it as an example to share with children, so that you can help them to see what they might strive for as writers. (2) Use it to determine next steps for each child by asking yourself, "What does this child need to practice as a writer if she is going to begin to write at the level of this benchmark piece?"

For conferring with individual students, it is probably most helpful if you study a piece of writing that is just one step higher than the writing he or she is already producing. For example, the Common Core State Standards expect that the benchmark for informational writing in June of kindergarten include naming a topic and then supplying information about the topic. A child who is still at the nonrepresentational stage, who (when asked) changes the meaning of the drawing from day to day, will more likely be working toward the mid-year benchmark rather than the June benchmark, until those drawings begin to look more like the objects they are intended to represent and the pages in the book stick to one main topic.

As you move about the room to confer today (and every day) you will want to refer to your school's end-of-year benchmarks and have those in the back of your mind as you make decisions about what to teach next for each child or group of children.

MID-WORKSHOP TEACHING **Writers Look Back through Old Work to be Sure They've Finished All They Can**

"Writers, eyes on me for a moment. Grace just did something that we can all learn from. She finished her how-to book and read it over. She made a couple of revisions using all that she knows about making her writing easy to read. And *then* she went back to a bunch of other pieces in her folder and did the same thing! You know what she discovered? There were some pieces in her folder that she'd forgotten to finish! She was kind of surprised. Sometimes when writers write a lot of different books, like you all do, you can lose track of what's done and what's not done. Before writing time is over today, make sure you check through your folders and see if you can find books that need to be finished that you might have forgotten about. If you don't have time to finish them, you could put them in the front of one of your folder pockets to remind you to finish them another time. Great work, Grace, and everyone!"

Celebrating Finishing the Class How-To Book

Celebrate finishing the class how-to book with a relevant song.

As soon as children were gathered for the share session at the meeting area, I invited kids to join in singing a new song. "Will you all sing along with me? I thought this song might be great way to celebrate the fact that we have finished our class how-to book. I think you will all enjoy this song. I think you'll see why."

Peanut! Peanut butter—and jelly! Peanut! Peanut butter—and jelly!

First you take the peanuts, and you dig them. Dig them. (Children repeat.)

Then you take the shells, and you crack them. Crack them.

Next, you take the peanuts, and you mash them. Mash them.

Then you take the bread, and you spread it. Spread it.

Peanut! Peanut butter—and jelly! Peanut! Peanut butter—and jelly!

Next, you take the grapes, and you pick them. Pick them.

Then you take the grapes, and you squish them. Squish them.

Then you take the bread, and you spread it. Spread it.

Now, you take the sandwich, and you eat it!

Dig them! Crack them! Mash them! Spread it! Mmmmmm Mmmmmm looks good.

Pick them! Squish them! Spread it! And eat it! Tastes good.

Peanut! Peanut butter—and jelly!

"Wow! This song is so much fun, isn't it? Not only is it about peanut butter and jelly, just like our class book, but it's also a how-to! It has steps, directions for doing something. It even has a conclusion!

"Speaking of peanut butter and jelly, I am so excited that we finally finished our class book. In fact, I think our book is so good that other kindergarten teachers might want to borrow it so they can teach their kids how to write how-to books just like us. Could you guys help me make some Post-its to label some of the most important things we learned about how-to books, so that the other kindergarten teachers can share that with their kids?" The kids were ready. (See Figure 16–1 on page 125.)

How to Make a Peanut Butter and Jelly Sandwich

Yummy, yummy. Do you want to make something yummy? A peanut butter and jelly sandwich is a delicious and easy to make sandwich made with bread, peanut butter, and jelly.

1. Get the jar of peanut butter. Be sure that you don't drop the jar.

2. Open it, and using your knife, scoop out a knife-full of peanut butter. Be sure the knife is clean.

3. Spread the peanut butter over one piece of bread

4. Open the jelly jar and use your knife to scoop out some jelly.

5. Spread the jelly over the other piece of bread.

6. Squish the two pieces of bread together. Make sure the peanut butter and jelly are on the inside!

Now you can make a peanut butter and jelly sandwich.

"Great. Turn and tell your partner one important thing about how-to books that we've learned, and then I'll make some Post-its to show where we did it in our peanut butter and jelly book. Go."

As kids spoke with their partners about some of the things they had learned so far in the unit, I circulated and wrote some of their ideas on Post-its. I added in a few of my own along the way.

"Writers, eyes up here. As you were all talking, I jotted down some of the great tips for how-to writing that you were sharing. Jarrett said he learned that how-to books have to have steps, so I wrote 'Steps' on this Post-it. Jarret, will you come up and put this Post-it on one of the places where our how-to book has steps?"

I shared a few other Post-its, designed to highlight some of the elements of how-to writing that I most wanted kids to be thinking about. "Someone said we learned to use warnings and tips. I'm going to stick that Post-it right here, where it says 'Be sure you don't drop the jar.'"

After a few minutes we had labeled five or six key features of our how-to text, reflecting on all that the children had learned in the unit. "Wow, thanks, kindergartners. The other teachers are going to be so excited to share this with their kids, to help them all learn how to write how-to books just like us!"

How-To Books Make Wonderful Gifts!

IN THIS SESSION, you'll teach students that to prepare for publishing, writers determine a specific audience for a piece of writing and dedicate that piece to that person.

GETTING READY

✔ At least one how-to book that contains a dedication (such as Alyssa Capucilli's *My First Soccer Game*) (see Connection)

✔ A blank sheet of dedication paper, as well as a small supply at each table to get children started, plus more at the writing center (see Teaching)

✔ Students' writing folders (see Active Engagement)

✔ Special star-shaped Post-its (or some other special material) for marking the piece chosen for publication (see Mid-Workshop Teaching)

✔ Individual copies of the Information Writing Checklists as well as an enlarged copy (see Share)

✔ "How-to Writing" chart (see Share)

✔ "Learning from a Mentor How-To Text" chart (see Share)

ARLIER IN THE UNIT, we suggested taking a look around at home to find examples of how-to books from your life. Truth is, not every how-to book is written down. Are you one of the lucky people who learned to cook without a recipe? Or maybe you know how to knit or fix a car or build a bookcase or identify birds or ride a horse or plant a garden without having every step written out for you. We all have been given the gift of knowing how to do things, whether we realized it at the time or not.

Your kindergartners are quite used to the role of receiving the gift of how-to teaching. When you are young, people are constantly teaching you things. For the remainder of the unit, your kindergartners will get to experience the other side. They will give the gift of how-to teaching by dedicating their how-to books to people they think will appreciate them. They might write brand-new how-to books especially for the people who matter most to them: family, friends, or maybe even pets. They can go back to how-to books they've already written and revise these a bit to turn them into more personalized gifts. Perhaps a number of children will decide to write for the same person—a favorite teacher, the principal, or a classmate. They might work together, collaborating to make a whole collection of how-to books for some lucky recipient.

If you haven't already done so, you'll want to announce that soon, the whole class will be publishing some of their how-to books and that publishing means people will be reading what they have created! It's a wonderful thing to mark the publishing date on the calendar and begin counting down the days. This not only builds enthusiasm for the approaching celebration, but also implicitly teaches a bit of time-management. Children, like many adults, will understand that every minute of writing workshop is precious, especially when there are just a few days left. Knowing how much time (or how little time) is available is often a great motivator, especially when the audience and purpose matter.

COMMON CORE STATE STANDARDS: W.K.2, W.K.5, RI.K.1, SL.K.1, L.K.1, L.K.2

How-To Books Make Wonderful Gifts!

CONNECTION

Using a personal example, explain that how-to books make wonderful gifts and can be dedicated to a particular reader.

"Writers, a few years ago, a friend of mine gave me one of the best gifts I have ever received. She knew that I love to cook, so she wrote down all her favorite family recipes and put them in a binder for me. She made a homemade recipe book for me! Can you believe that? Do you want to see?" I held up the recipe book, a homemade collection of hand-written recipes. "Look what she did. She even took photos of some of the cakes and cookies so that I could see what they would look like when they were done!" The kids oohed and ahhed over some of the tasty-looking sweets.

"Here's another thing I wanted to show you. My friend is not the only person who gives how-to books as gifts. Take a look. These how-to books have something called *dedications*. A *dedication* is like a message that says 'This book is for. . . .' It lets people know who you think would really love your book." I opened up *My First Soccer Game*. "Check it out. Even Alyssa Satin Capucilli has a dedication! It says, 'For the Shadowlawn soccer stars!' and she signed it with her initials, A.S.C. And there's another dedication: 'To my dad, Ben, who coached me to shoot a soccer ball as well as with a camera!' The photographer wrote that dedication. So you see, a dedication is like giving the book to somebody as a gift. It's like Alyssa is giving this book to the Shadowlawn soccer stars, whoever they are. And the photographer is giving this book to her dad."

❖ Name the teaching point.

"Writers, today I want to teach you that how-to books make amazing gifts. Writers often write books for people they care about or for people they would like to teach. Writers often write dedications for those people, to let everybody know who the book was really written for."

◆ COACHING

Oftentimes we bring experiences from our own lives into our writing workshop. It helps our students feel connected to us and also drives home the point that just as they do, we live our lives as writers as well. If you don't have a how-to gift, such as the one we describe here, simply telling a story about somebody who has taught you something will suffice.

TEACHING

Think aloud as you weigh various dedication possibilities and tuck in tips for choosing a recipient that makes sense.

"Let's try this: we'll turn our book, 'How to Make a Peanut Butter and Jelly Sandwich,' into a gift. Who could we give this how-to book to? Who would really appreciate this book, or who would really be able to use this book? Let me think.

"How about the principal? No, probably not. I happen to know that she is allergic to peanuts, so this would not be a very good gift for her. It's a good thing I thought of that! It helps to think about what you know about the person before you dedicate the book to her.

"Let's see if I can think of somebody who actually likes to eat PB&Js but might not know how to make them." I pretended to be deep in thought and made it clear that the kids should be thinking along with me. "Hey! I know. How about we dedicate this book to our friends in K-102 across the hall? They would love this book, because not only do they love peanut butter and jellies, they also love how-to books! They've been writing them too!" The kids squealed "Yeah!" and it was decided.

Model writing a dedication page.

"Now, all that is left to do is to write the dedication." I held up a special page of paper created just for writing dedications, a simple page with just a few lines surrounded by plenty of white space. "This paper will be at the writing center for the rest of the unit, so that you can write dedications for your how-to books. Writing a dedication is kind of like writing a card to go with a gift." I pointed to the lines on the page and gestured to where the writing would go, "A dedication can say, 'To . . .' and 'From . . . ,' and sometimes the dedication can even include a little bit about why the book is dedicated to that particular person. What do you think we could write for our dedication?" I paused to give kids a chance to think along with me (mostly to support engagement) and then moved on. "Okay, I think I'll write 'Dedicated to K-102, a class who loves how-to books as much as we do! From K-106.'" I quickly wrote the dedication down and attached the new page to our class how-to book.

"What do you all think? It's a pretty nice dedication, isn't it? If I were K-102, I would definitely be excited to receive this gift."

ACTIVE ENGAGEMENT

Encourage students to choose one of their how-to books and decide to whom it will be dedicated.

"Now it's your turn. This time, I'd like you to pick one of your how-to books. Then decide whom you might dedicate it to. Try to think of somebody that might be interested in your topic or might not know how to do what you are teaching. Ready? Take out one of your how-to books now."

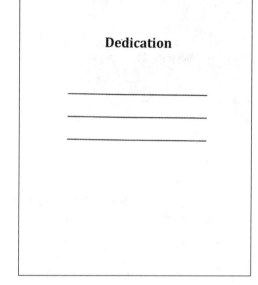

A sample of paper students might use for writing their dedications. Children may also design their own using blank paper.

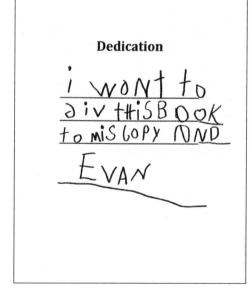

I want to give this book to Miss Jopy and Evan.

FIG. 17–1

As kids worked, I voiced over, "Maybe you'll dedicate your book to somebody who just loves to read how-to books. I know *I* love to read how-to books, I'd love to have a how-to dedicated to me!"

LINK

Rally students to try today's work in the context of ongoing writing work.

"I see that most of you have decided on somebody to give your how-to book to as a gift, and you are ready to write dedications. This is a huge day for us, actually, because this is something that grown-up writers *really do*. I really do use this recipe book that my friend made for me, and it really is one of the best gifts that I have ever received. In fact, how-to books are just one kind of writing that you can give as a gift, and I hope that after today, all of you will always think of making books for people whenever a birthday or a holiday comes up or whenever you just want to surprise somebody or make them feel good.

"For most of you, writing a dedication for one book is not going to take very long. So you have many choices. You might want to go back to all of your how-to books and write a dedication for each one to somebody who would really like to receive that book as a gift. You might decide to make a new how-to book from scratch today, especially for somebody—just like my friend made this recipe book especially for me because she knew that I love to cook."

Build students' energy for the approaching end of the unit.

"Soon, we will be finishing up the unit. Today is the last day that you'll really have time to start any new books, so it's especially important to write as much as you can today!" I pointed to the class calendar. "Two days from now is the day that we'll be having our publishing party. On that day we're going to have guests come into the classroom so that you can share all the great work you've done in this unit. You'll read one favorite how-to book to a small group of visitors, and we'll also go on a special walk around the school to bring your how-to books to people around the school. You might even mail a how-to book to someone you want to have it. That means you only have two more days to make one of your how-to books extra special, to share at the celebration and then give it to somebody as a gift."

By naming yourself as a lover of how-to books, and as a potential dedicatee, you're giving every kid in your class an automatic possibility while leaving the door open to dedicate their books to whomever they wish.

By showing students the approaching end of the unit, I am not only building excitement for the celebration, but also making it clear that a deadline is nearing.

Supporting Students as They Revise Books Selected for Publication

IN TODAY'S MID-WORKSHOP TEACHING POINT, you asked kids to choose one how-to book to share at the publishing party. With the end of the unit fast approaching, you will want to begin pulling aside groups and individuals who need support finishing up the pieces they have chosen for publication. You'll want to teach some groups of children that published authors rarely, if ever, publish the first draft of something they wrote. Rather, they reread, thinking carefully about what else they might add to make their writing more detailed or how they might say things more clearly. You might teach kids to look back once again at all of the charts from the unit and check to be sure they considered every possible strategy for making their published piece of writing shine. You will certainly want to emphasize that crossed-out chunks are a badge of honor, something to be proud of as a writer. You'll want to seek out the kids in your classroom who are strong "revisers" and hold up their crossed-out lines, rewritten parts, and added on strips and pages as examples, saying to the others, "Wow! Look at how much revision this person did! Look at all that work. That is the sign of somebody who is really thinking hard about their writing and is trying to make their writing the best that it can be."

This does not mean the piece they choose will need to be perfect. Clearly, publishing in a kindergarten classroom is not the same as publishing in the adult world of writing. The message you want to transmit to your students is that the hard work of writing is what matters most here: drafting, revising, then drafting and revising again and again and again. You will also want to be sure kids get the message that doing it on their own, independently, is more desirable than relying heavily on teacher support to create a "polished" product.

The spelling and handwriting will be reflective of what your kindergartners actually do know about spelling at this point in time. Kindergartners will not waste time doing the labor-intensive and time-consuming work of recopying to achieve a perfect end-product. Instead, your publishing celebration will celebrate the challenging process that your children have been engaged in all along. You will want to shine a spotlight on kids who made big revisions to their work, children who tried and tried again, kids who worked hard, thought they couldn't make a how-to book, but in the end they did it!

MID-WORKSHOP TEACHING
Choosing a Piece to Give as a Gift

"Writers, please put your pens down and listen very carefully." I waited until every set of eyes was on me. "Right now we're going to do something very important. We're going to choose a piece to share at the publishing party that we're having at the end of the week! I want to give you a few tips for picking a piece.

"First, pick a piece that you want to give as a gift to someone or put on display in the school somewhere, because that's going to be part of the party. Each of you will get to put your how-to book on display anywhere in the building you want (well, almost), or put your how-to book in the mail to send to somebody as a present." I paused to let that sink in for a moment and then continued. "So when you choose your piece, you're also choosing the *reader* you want it to go to—the reader that you think will learn the most from it. I'm going to be coming around soon and making a list of where your pieces are going to go so that I can send envelopes home with those of you who want to mail them—so you can bring in the addresses.

"Second, I recommend that you choose a piece that you enjoy working on because we still have the rest of today and tomorrow to continue working just on that one piece of writing. I don't think you will want to a pick a piece that you look at and think, 'I am done.' Instead pick a piece that you look at and think, 'Oh, I know what I could change.'

"At each of your tables are some special star-shaped Post-its. There are enough for each of you to take one and stick it on to the special how-to book you have chosen. Tonight, I'm going to empty out your folders so that tomorrow, when you open up your folder, the only how-to book left in it is going to be the book you chose for the publishing party. Right now, everybody, read through your how-to books and mark the one you want to keep working on with your special star-shaped Post-it."

Self-Assessment and Goal Setting

Channel students to use their Information Writing Checklist to check their goals for the piece they plan to celebrate.

"Writers, today I'd like you to come to the meeting area carrying only the how-to book that you marked with a special star-shaped Post-it for publishing and your little Information Writing Checklist." As I called children group by group to the carpet, I checked to see that they each had these two things.

"Writers, this is an exciting day! Think about how much you have learned since the beginning of the unit! Remember the things you learned about how-to writing when we first started studying it?" I pointed to where our first "How-To Writing" chart was hanging. "And remember all of the things you learned from studying other authors' how-to books?" I pointed to the chart "Learning from a Mentor How-To Text." "And do you remember the Information Writing Checklist, the one you've used before to check on your goals? Phew, that is a lot of new learning in one unit!"

 I pointed to the Information Writing Checklist that I had displayed on the easel next to me. The children had their individual copies of this chart in their laps along with their how-to books.

As you read through the Information Writing Checklist, ask students to indicate which goals they have met.

"Writers, I asked you to bring your little Information Writing Checklists to the rug because I think that now is a good time to check in on the goals that you set for yourselves. Right now, look at your own Information Writing Checklist. A

Information Writing Checklist

	Kindergarten	NOT YET	STARTING TO	YES!	Grade 1	NOT YET	STARTING TO	YES!
	Structure				**Structure**			
Overall	I told, drew, and wrote about a topic.	☐	☐	☐	I taught my readers about a topic.	☐	☐	☐
Lead	I told what my topic was.	☐	☐	☐	I named my topic in the beginning and got my readers' attention.	☐	☐	☐
Transitions	I put different things I knew about the topic on my pages.	☐	☐	☐	I told different parts about my topic on different pages.	☐	☐	☐
Ending	I had a last part or page.	☐	☐	☐	I wrote an ending.	☐	☐	☐
Organization	I told, drew, and wrote information across pages.	☐	☐	☐	I told about my topic part by part.	☐	☐	☐
	Development				**Development**			
Elaboration	I drew and wrote important things about the topic.	☐	☐	☐	I put facts in my writing to teach about my topic.	☐	☐	☐
Craft	I told, drew, and wrote some details about the topic.	☐	☐	☐	I used labels and words to give facts.	☐	☐	☐
	Language Conventions				**Language Conventions**			
Spelling	I could read my writing.	☐	☐	☐	I used all I knew about words and chunks (*at, op, it,* etc.) to help me spell.	☐	☐	☐
	I wrote a letter for the sounds I heard.	☐	☐	☐	I spelled the word wall words right and used the word wall to help me spell other words.	☐	☐	☐
	I used the word wall to help me spell.	☐	☐	☐				

This checklist can be found on the CD-Rom.

while back, you each placed a star next to the thing you said you really wanted to work on. Some of you chose to put different things that you know about your topic on the pages. Thumbs up if that is what you picked. Some of you chose to tell, draw, and write some details about your topic. Thumbs up if that is you." I continued down the list, giving kids a chance to give a thumbs up for each of the items. "Right now, please find a place in your writing where it shows that you worked on your goal. Put your finger on a spot that shows that you worked on your goal. Take your time." I waited as children reread their how-to books. Some children right away pointed to their titles or specific words or lines in their writing. I circulated, noting where children were pointing in the booklets and whether it matched what they had marked on their Information Writing Checklists. I jotted down the names of the few children that couldn't find a spot to point to and made a mental note to meet with them tomorrow.

"Right now, turn to your partner and share what you put your finger on and why you put your finger on that spot." Again, I circulated, listening in. In some cases I swooped by, asking probing questions or prompting kids to say more.

"Wow! I am so impressed with the way you are all thinking carefully about your goals as writers. In fact, I think that the thing I am most impressed with is that many of you still want to keep on working on some of these things. So many of you said, 'Even though I worked on this and I got better at it, I think there is even more that I could try.' Wow. Give yourselves a pat on the back!"

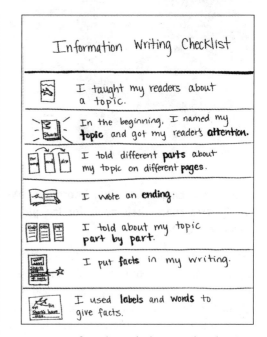

FIG. 17–2   If you haven't done so already, you may want to hang an enlarged, handmade version of the first-grade Information Writing Checklist alongside the one for kindergarten. You'll want to be sure that any children who are ready to check their work using the first-grade chart also have typed small versions of their own.

Preparing for the Publishing Party
Writers Do Their Best Work Now to Share It Later

YOUR KINDERGARTEN WRITERS have learned a lot about making their writing easy to read. Since they first came to kindergarten, they have grown immeasurably in their knowledge of conventions and mechanics. Of course, writing workshop is only one component of a balanced literacy program that provides opportunities for students to practice conventions, and you'll have been building many other opportunities for this kind of work across your days as well.

As mentioned earlier, it is only natural when we've focused several lessons on the craft of writing how-to books, for kindergartners to pay less attention to incorporating all that they are learning about using conventions. As we approach the end of the unit and prepare for publication and celebration, it is important to remind students about all that they know not only about the craft of writing how-to books, but about how to make their writing easy for readers to read. It is helpful to establish that rereading with an eye on conventions—making writing easy for readers to read—is an important part of preparing to share our writing with the larger community.

As your young writers prepare to publish one of their how-to books, you will want to take this opportunity to teach them how to use an editing checklist. The checklist will not introduce new skills, but will serve as a concrete reminder of all that they've learned about making writing easier for readers to read. Using an editing checklist will remind students to incorporate these things into their published pieces—and all of their writing. (By this point, students have grown accustomed to checklists of all kinds, so editing checklists will not feel unfamiliar.) After introducing this tool to your students, you can keep a stack in the writing center so students can use them regularly.

You are the one best positioned to decide what goes on an editing checklist based on what you know of your students and what you've taught them. You might decide that your particular class of writers is ready to include ending punctuation, or that your class is still working toward using upper- and lowercase letters conventionally and that it doesn't make sense to include end punctuation on an editing checklist. The most important thing is that you create an editing checklist tailored just for them.

IN THIS SESSION, you'll teach students that writers use an editing checklist to prepare their writing for publication.

GETTING READY

✔ Student writing folders containing how-to books that they have chosen for celebration (see Connection)

✔ One popsicle stick pointer for each child (placed in each child's writing folder). Each end of the popsicle stick should have a different-colored sticker on it (or a different-colored dot made with marker). You will need to have prepared this ahead of time. Alternatively, you can choose to use two different-colored crayons (see Teaching).

✔ An enlarged copy of the editing checklists as well as individual copies for all children, tucked into their writing folders, with extras in the writing center (see Teaching).

✔ Demonstration piece, "How to Make a Peanut Butter and Jelly Sandwich," or text that has been used as demonstration text all along (see Teaching)

✔ Pens that are a different color from the tool children have been using for writing their booklets (see Active Engagement)

✔ You will want to collect any addressed envelopes children bring in to prepare for the celebration.

COMMON CORE STATE STANDARDS: W.K.2, W.K.5, W.K.6, RFS.K.1, RFS.K.3, SL.K.1, SL.K.6, L.K.1, L.K.2

Preparing for the Publishing Party
Writers Do Their Best Work Now to Share It Later

CONNECTION

Explain that students now have three jobs. They are already writers and teachers, and today they also become editors who have the job of making sure their writing is easy for readers to read.

After making sure the children had a little extra room to spread out this morning, I called them to the meeting area with their writing folders, which at this point had only the piece chosen for publication inside. "Writers, as soon as you sit down, you can take out the how-to books you are going to share at the celebration."

"The grown-ups who take care of you have several jobs. They are parents, they are food shoppers, and they might have different jobs they go to during the day, as well. Just like the grown-ups in your lives, *you* have lots of different jobs. You are sons and daughters, students, and teachers, too! Let's think of all the jobs that you already have in our classroom. Thumbs up if you are a writer. Thumbs up if you are a teacher. How about mathematician? Scientist?" Thumbs popped up all around. "Well, today, we are going to add another job. You are going to be editors! This is a big and important job. An editor has the responsibility of making sure that writing is easy for readers to read!"

❧ **Name the teaching point.**

"Today I want to teach you that you can be an editor and edit your own writing to make sure it's easy for readers to read. You can use our new editing checklist to make sure you used capital letters at the beginning of each sentence and lowercase letters for the rest of the letters in words, and that you spelled word wall words correctly."

TEACHING

Prepare students to use the editing checklist and popsicle stick pointers you have prepared.

"Writers, today when you open your writing folder, you will find a surprise, but don't look yet. Let's all do it together. When I say the word *editors*, open your folder, and then you can look. Ready . . . editors." As children opened their folders and took out the pointers, their excitement was palpable.

"These are not just any old popsicle sticks. They have been made into editing pointers, and are going to help us edit our writing," I continued. "Are you ready for me to show you how they can help you do this important work? Let's look at the first thing on our checklist." I turned to the enlarged copy of the editing checklist, pointed to the first line (checking

◆ COACHING

It is important for young children to understand that editing is a natural part of the writing process, and that they now are ready to assume this responsibility.

for upper- and lowercase letters), and said, "The red dot on this side of the popsicle stick is in charge of checking for upper- and lowercase letters."

Demonstrate how to use the popsicle stick pointer to check for one element of the editing checklist, and ask students to give it a try.

"Let me show you how I check my writing with the magic editing pointer." I held up a copy of "How to Make a Peanut Butter and Jelly Sandwich," and I placed my popsicle stick directly under the first letter of the first word. "Uppercase *G*," I said, thinking aloud. "Yes. I remembered to use a capital letter at the beginning." I moved the popsicle stick to the next letter. "Yes, lowercase *e*," I said as I moved the stick along. I continued to do this for all the words in the first sentence.

"Now, your turn. Get your book ready. Take your stick with the red dot at the end and check for uppercase and lowercase letters. Begin with the first letter of the first word. Remember that should be an uppercase letter. Then move your pointer along until you check all the letters in all the words." After about a minute, I added, "Take your pen and change any letters you find that need to be changed."

ACTIVE ENGAGEMENT

Ask children to use their editing pointers to check for the next item on the editing checklist; in this case, checking for word wall words—word by word, page by page.

"Writers, our editing checklist tells us that we have one more thing we need to do. Flip your popsicle stick to the blue circle on the other side, and use that side to find word wall words and make sure they're spelled just the way they look on the word wall. Check now for your word wall words by moving your stick with the blue circle along, word by word and page by page. When you come to a word wall word, if you notice that it is not spelled correctly, take your special editing pen and change it." I saw heads bobbing up and down as children raised and lowered their eyes to check and double-check their words. I moved around the group, complimenting all the editing that I saw happening.

Convene the class and compliment children on their editing work.

I convened the class. "Congratulations. The magic editing pointer helped you become great detectives. You fixed up lots of word wall words, and you found places in your writing where you used uppercase letters instead of lowercase letters, and you fixed those places too! Great editors are always great detectives."

LINK

Review the editing checklist and remind children that they can use this with any piece of writing.

"So from now on, writers, teachers, and editors, any time you are finished with a piece of writing, take out your editing checklist and be your own editor. You will find editing checklists in the writing center and in your writing folder to remind you. You can take your magic popsicle stick and use it to help you. If you want your book to teach people how to do something, they need to be able to read it, and this is one way to make your writing easier to read."

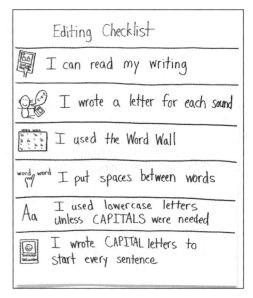

FIG. 18–1 Picture support helps children understand this checklist. You may also decide to adapt or eliminate some of the items.

Introduction

Introduction: Hey, is it boring with old games and you want to learn to play Lazertag? Then this book is good for you. Even for babies.

Things You Need...

Things you need... Lazer gun, Lazer shirt, Lazer pants, shirt, Lazertag place that you can visit nearby, Players, Parent's supervision

Step 1

Step 1: First drive to the Lazertag place. Ask your mom to go! She will drive, not you!

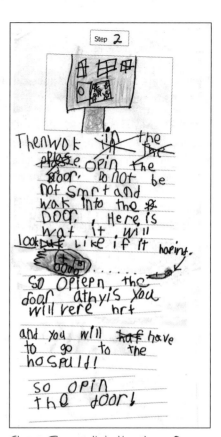

Step 2

Step 2: Then walk in the place. Open the door. Do not be not smart and walk into the door. Here is what it will look like if it happened. So open the door or else you will [get] very hurt and you will have to go to the hospital! So open the door!

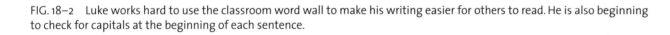

FIG. 18–2 Luke works hard to use the classroom word wall to make his writing easier for others to read. He is also beginning to check for capitals at the beginning of each sentence.

Step 3: Then the worker will bring you to Lazertag. Make sure that you are with the worker.

FIG. 18–2 (Continued)

Step 4: Then you have to put on your vest.

Step 5: Then another worker will put you in the arena.

Final Words: Now you know how to play Lazertag. I hope you like it it is really fun for me maybe it will for you. Have fun! Yay you like it!

Differentiating the Final Work of the Unit

ON THIS DAY, RIGHT BEFORE THE CELEBRATION, your conferring and small-group work will fall into three main categories. The first focuses on supporting children who need extra support, the second is supporting students who are ready to move beyond the minilesson, and the third is helping students practice for the celebration by acting out their how-to books.

Christian fell into the first category. Before I began the conference, I noticed that he had written several things that had been crossed out. Christian often took each minilesson to heart, and sometimes that meant he put so much importance on one feature, he'd get stuck and have a hard time moving on. I suspected that this was happening today.

"What's going on, Christian?" I asked as I knelt down by him. "I noticed that you had several ideas that you crossed out at the beginning of your book about how to make a snowman, and now you seem stuck."

"Yeah. I don't know who to do. My dad taught me how to make a snowman, but so did my friend Nicholas. So I don't know." Christian trailed off and shrugged. It seemed like his current solution was to sit and wait.

"Don't worry! You can write your dedication to two people. Either you can write two dedication pages, with one person on each page or you can write both of them on the same page. Writers do that all the time. Will that help solve your problem?" I asked. He shook his head yes and started writing. Problem solved! Sometimes it just takes a small nudge to help a stuck writer get unstuck and move forward. Before moving on, I said, "Any time you are stuck on something, ask yourself, 'What's my problem, and what can I do to solve my problem?' And if you can't find an answer to that question, try asking your writing partner for some advice."

To address the needs of writers in the second category, you might convene a small group focused on enriching today's convention-focused minilesson. There will always be writers who are ready to move forward. You probably will find that there are children that are ready to learn about capitalization of the first letter of a proper noun or children that are ready to learn about punctuation. Some will be ready just for periods at the end of a sentence, while a few others will be ready for other kinds of punctuation marks: question marks and exclamation points.

And to address the needs of writers in the third category—writers who have finished writing, revising, and editing—you might convene a small group of writers and rally them to begin practicing reading their writing and acting it out, preparing for tomorrow's celebration. A few of these children will be able to demonstrate this at the onset of the share session so all children have a vision of what they are moving toward.

MID-WORKSHOP TEACHING
Writers Add On to Their Own Checklists

"Writers, eyes on me," I said, standing in my regular place in the center of the room. "Lexi was editing her writing just now, and she noticed that she forgot to put in periods at the end of sentences. So she went back on each page, and she added periods at the end of every sentence. Then Lexi did another smart thing. She added something else onto her editing checklist. She just wrote it right on! Can you guess what?" I paused a second, waiting for the students to answer. "Periods. Yes, that's right! You can do that too."

Reading Aloud

Organize students to practice reading and acting out their how-to books in preparation for the next day's celebration.

Children gathered in the meeting area with the how-to books they'd chosen to publish. I said, "Writers, I saw each of you doing the important work of editors today, using your editing pointers and editing checklists to make your writing easy to read. Some of you even came up with more things to add to the checklist! That's great. We're almost ready for tomorrow's celebration! When writers are getting ready to share their writing with readers, they practice reading it out loud the best they can—and even act it out! Reading your writing out loud is like a performance, and when you're getting ready to perform something, you practice it over and over again, right? With how-to books, writers decide on places where they can out act the directions. They decide on places they are going to read with a loud voice and other places they will read with a quiet voice. And they read it again and again and again so their voice is smooth, just like they do when they are reading their books for reading workshop. Our share session today is going to last a little bit longer, since each one of you will have a turn to practice reading your writing, getting ready for our celebration. In a minute, you're going to spread out and find a place where you can practice reading and acting out your how-to book on your own, and then I'm going to call you together in groups of two partnerships so you can practice with a bigger audience."

Publishing Celebration
Writers Are Teachers!

Dear Teachers,

Today's writing workshop is an invitation to come to the celebration! The work your students have done in this unit is incredibly important. Not only have they been learning about writing how-to books, they have been building foundational skills that are the basis of all the informational writing they will study and write in years to come. They have learned the unique characteristics of a new genre, how-to books, while continuing to practice skills that enrich their writing work in any genre. They have built stamina as well, writing longer books with pages that have several steps. Most importantly, perhaps, they have become confident in the understanding that they can teach readers through their writing. This celebration day will be particularly meaningful then, perhaps, because the room will brim with real readers just waiting to learn from your students!

In her book *I'm in Charge of Celebrations*, Bird Baylor (1995) lets us know that the simplest things in life are causes for celebration. She writes, "You can tell what's worth a celebration because your heart will POUND and you'll feel like you're standing on top of a mountain and you'll catch your breath like you were breathing some new kind of air." In this unit, your children have been breathing the air of how-to writing, living and thinking and writing like teachers—and this is certainly worth a celebration. Your students have come to understand that at the end of every unit, there is a celebration. What marks this unit as unique is that for the first time, your students will have made a book designed specifically to teach readers something new. As always, there are many ways to publish and celebrate, and it's important in this case to design a celebration that will give students an opportunity to use their writing to teach readers. Remember, it is not the celebration itself that should be the focus of your attention, but rather all the work that went into making these wonderful how-to books. As always, you'll choose something that makes sense for you and your students.

One exciting option is to record video of each student reading and when possible demonstrating his or her published piece. This can be accomplished relatively easily by inviting a parent or volunteer to come into your classroom during writing workshop for the last few days of the unit to pull one student aside at a time. For the publishing party, the whole class, and if you choose, some invited guests, can sit back and watch a compilation of these short clips. You can even burn DVD copies for parents and caregivers who aren't available during the school day. If your school has a website, you could link to the how-to book videos through that. This is an authentic way for students to share their work in today's media-driven world.

Of course, if you prefer, having students read their books in person to an audience of caregivers or peers is a wonderful option. As we describe below, a real-life audience is so important to young writers—to every writer! We take it a step further. After students have shared their writing with the general audience group, we make time for them to prepare their how-to books to be sent into the world, aimed toward the particular audience they feel will be helped the most by the books they have created.

A LETTER TO FAMILIES

Your child has spent several weeks writing books that teach people how to do something. He or she has written about many different topics. You may have been hearing your child talk about this work at home. The students have spent lots of time thinking about all of the things they know how to do that they could teach other people about—things like baseball, baking chocolate chip cookies, planting seeds, taking care of younger siblings. The expertise of these young writers goes on and on!

This is a particularly big unit in your child's writing life. It is his or her first immersion in the world of informational writing. Perfecting the art of informational writing is an incredibly important life skill, and it is also a big emphasis of the new Common Core State Standards. This unit fosters a lot of the listening and speaking skills that are built into the new standards as well. And the work of this unit will not end with our upcoming celebration. Your child will continue to find opportunities to teach others and to write how-to books about all that he or she knows how to do. You can help keep this work going. If you are going food shopping with your child, for example, you might want to emphasize the steps involved. If your child builds a Lego house, ask him or her to tell you the steps involved. Don't be surprised to see your child run to get paper to write it down! Having paper on hand at home can encourage this.

You can also help your child be on the lookout for how-to writing: When you go to the Post Office to mail a package, read the directions on the mailer to your child. When shopping online, read the directions step by step as you check out. When cooking, point out that recipes are just like how-to books!

Welcome to the world of informational writing! The children and I can't wait to share with you.

PREPARATION

Invite guests to arrive about half an hour after writers arrive in class, allowing time for the children to get settled. Children will have practiced reading and acting out their booklets prior to this day and will have taken a seat on their names taped to the rug or floor. Place the topic chart on the front door leading to the classroom so everyone coming in will see the vast expertise of the young writers in the room!

THE CELEBRATION

As with all classroom celebrations, you'll want to send the signal to students that this day is different. You might meet students in the school yard a little earlier than usual, and say, "I know that you are wondering why I am here early. I couldn't wait to see you. I bet that you are as excited as I am for our writing celebration and to teach other people how to do what you know how to do so well. Come on, let's be the first ones to get to class."

As you walk, you might tell your writers how you were so excited you couldn't sleep last night and that you know some of them had the same feeling. On reaching the classroom, show children the topic chart that has been placed on the front door. Let children know that today they are not only celebrating their writing, but they are also celebrating teaching others. After the children have looked at the chart for a moment, invite them into the classroom to quickly pick up their how-to books and find their spots on the floor to wait for the guests. As they walk into the classroom, have "Hokey Pokey" and/or "Bunny Hop" and/or "Peanut Butter and Jelly" or any other song that gives instructions for how to do something playing in the background.

As guests begin to arrive, invite them to sit down next to a writer. Students will begin reading or acting out their how-to books as soon as they have an audience. Encourage visitors to move along to other children when one child has finished, so everyone has a chance to share with a reader. You may want to interrupt at some point when most of the guests have arrived, to welcome them and explain how the celebration is working. The more listeners each student has, the better, so remind visitors to keep moving so that they can hear as many how-to books as possible. Also remind children to use their best acting-out voices.

Ask guests to leave compliments on a slip of paper for each child, so all writers receive meaningful questions and suggestions from the adults and classmates who came to hear them read.

CELEBRATION WALK

After all students have finished reading and teaching (you will want to have made sure to leave time for the celebration walk as well), gather students into a circle. Thank the guests for coming and thank the writers for teaching the guests about their topics. Tell the guests that the writers are now going to go on a celebration walk and they are invited to join in.

Students will have previously decided where they'd like to place or send their books, and you'll have collected the addressed envelopes returned by those students who have decided to mail their how-to books to a particular reader. (Stamp the envelopes, or give the students the stamps to put on—fun!) Others will have determined a recipient in the school to hand-deliver their books to. Those students who are mailing their books may now fold them and put them in the envelopes. Other students may also put their books in envelopes, writing the name or location where the book is going. Ask any guests who can to stay for this part of the celebration to help escort writers to their destinations in the school. If many writers choose to mail their books to someone, you might save the school or corner mail box as the final stop. You may want to organize students into small groups to be led by volunteers to make the walk. The point is to give children the opportunity to get their how-to books in the hands of the specific readers they've written them for.

Let the celebration walk begin. Enjoy!

Lucy, Laurie and Beth

1. How to build Lego Darth Vader

2. Read this book to make Lego Darth Vader.

3. Head, Pants, Body, Mask, Cape

4. How to build Lego Darth Vader. Get a Lego head.

5. Get a Lego body and a Lego pants.

6. Get the Lego pants on. Get a Lego cape. Warning! Do not step on Lego! It hurts!

7. Put the cape on and get a Lego mask.

8. Put the mask on. That's how to make a Lego Darth Vader.

9. Thank you for reading this book.

10. I want to give this book to Miss Jopy and Evan.

FIG. 19–1   Kurt uses a full repertoire of strategies to write this book.

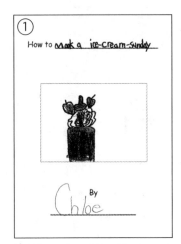

How to make an ice-cream sundae.

Do you like ice cream then read my book.

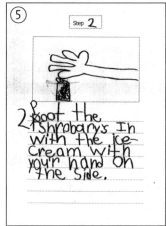

ice cream. cup. strawberries. whip cream. berry. bowl.

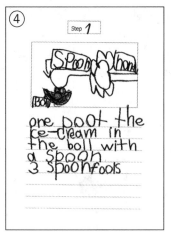

1. Put the ice cream in the bowl with a spoon 3 spoonfuls.

2. Put the strawberries in with the ice cream with your hand on the side.

3. Put the whip cream in with the other stuff.

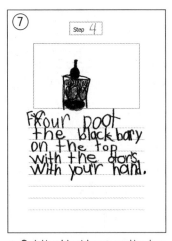

4. Put the blackberry on the top with the other's with your hand.

Eat it. Yum-yum-yum.

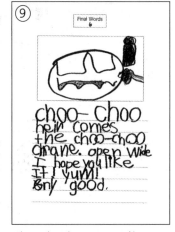

Choo-choo here comes the choo-choo train. Open wide. I hope you like it. Yum! Very good.

FIG. 19–2 Introductions and conclusions make the writing complete.